SUCCESSION PLANNING

FOR FAMILY BUSINESSES

A SUCCESSION PARADIGM™ BOOK

SUCCESSION PLANNING FOR FAMILY BUSINESSES

Preparing for the Next Generation

MICHAEL A. LOBRAICO

JONATHAN ISAACS

MITCHELL SINGER

Foreword by Thomas William Deans, Ph.D.

NEW YORK, TORONTO

Published in 2011 by
BPS Books
bpsbooks.com
Toronto and New York
A division of Bastian Publishing Services Ltd.

ISBN 978-1-926645-53-7

Cataloguing in Publication Data available from Library and Archives Canada

DISCLAIMER
The information contained herein is intended for information purposes only and is not intended to be a substitute for specific legal, accounting, tax, financial, or other advice or recommendations for any individual or business. The information may not be the most current or complete. Readers are advised to seek appropriate advice in the appropriate jurisdiction to which it may apply.

THE SUCCESSION PARADIGM™
The Succession Paradigm is a trademark of The Family Business Counsel of Canada. This book is an overview of the topic of succession planning for family businesses but is not a fait accompli solution in and of itself. Our resource and approach, The Succession Paradigm, is an integrated approach for family businesses and businesses needing to implement a structured process bringing them from the stage of fact finding to transition. This book will ideally be read and applied in conjunction with The Succession Paradigm program and the advice of The Family Business Counsel of Canada, 590 Alden Road, Unit 206-7, Markham, ON L3R 8N2 (905-305-9900); www.familybcc.com

CONTENTS

FOREWORD

You couldn't invent a more complex and fascinating subject to study than family businesses — they are the perfect intersection of money, family, control, love, trust, and respect. A family business, especially at its inception, represents all that is good about family. These enterprises are loaded with goodwill and optimism, but most of all they are brimming with the hope that hard work, in combination with family members working shoulder to shoulder, will create something magnificent and enduring.

What unfolds as time marches on in a family business often leaves so many feeling lesser and failed. It is precisely this potential for wealth destruction and family acrimony that Michael Lobraico, Jonathan Isaacs, and Mitchell Singer seek to help business owners avoid through their important contribution to the family business literature. That *Succession Planning for Family Business* is a collaborative effort by three authors with vastly different types of family business experience and areas of technical savvy speaks to both the complexity of the subject matter of this book and the value of its message.

As an unprecedented number of family business owners approach retirement, they are being confronted with the stark reality that their last deal — the transition of their business to a new owner — will be their most difficult deal of all. Many business owners will do what these seasoned family business experts have seen over and over — *nothing*. Doing nothing becomes the default plan for legions of family business owners. Why so many otherwise intelligent and hard-working entrepreneurs fail to plan for the most obvious progressions of life — incapacitation and death — is doubly tragic when you consider how difficult it will be for the surviving spouse and children to operate the business when the business owner is no longer there.

I have to say that I couldn't stop turning the pages when I read the draft manuscript, especially the section in which Michael Lobraico chronicles his own family business narrative. It takes extraordinary courage for any author to share personal anecdotes, but it is especially moving when the motivation is to help other families avoid the heartache that the author has himself endured. It is the honesty of this author's family business odyssey that gives readers a gift — an insight into how high the stakes can be when families fail to initiate and maintain open communication.

Too often family businesses paint a picture of multi-generational bliss even after family businesses have failed. That this book has been written in such a deliberate and honest voice speaks volumes about the character of the authors, who clearly desire to help families find their own way forward. Readers will see up close and personal that when family business succession is neglected, families will pay so profound a price that it transcends money and cuts right to the heart of why we work. Between the pages of this well-crafted book we learn that the central tenet of a thoughtful succession plan is a family that is built to last.

The authors have organized this book in a wise sequence. In Part 1, "Why You Need a Corporate Will," they tell a cautionary tale — the aforementioned Lobraico family business story. It is undeniably powerful. This sets the stage for a general overview of how succession planning works. The pragmatic nature of this assessment will leave readers thinking and believing that they, too, can master their family business universe — and that asking for help is the first step.

In Part 2 the authors transition the discussion into an engaging overview of how succession planning is carried out. The authors acknowledge the perception of business owners that succession planning is both complex and time consuming and offer a compelling case that in fact it doesn't need to be either. They rightly beat the drum for the idea that constant communication among all family members, including those outside the business, is essential. Silence is the great destroyer of wealth. It is the intent of this book to get families talking.

This part of the book offers another family business story — the hypothetical Blooms Floral story — and ties fascinating family business lessons and themes to the three-circle family business model. Readers will easily grasp how interconnected yet distinct management, ownership, and family are and how an understanding of their interplay is essential for families to successfully manage and transition their business.

It is noteworthy that every year billionaires die and leave their estate, their business, and their family in chaos. Readers who assume that the "success" in "succession" can be purchased are missing the point. Succession planning should be a collaborative exercise that brings family together to share individual and collective ideas about the future. In this new and important book, families in business together have an invaluable new resource to help them gather the courage and confidence to preserve their greatest and most enduring legacy — their family.

Tom Deans, Ph.D., author of
Every Family's Business: 12 Common Sense Questions to Protect Your Wealth

PREFACE

How can a family business ensure that both the family and the business are protected from one generation to another? How can it ensure that the resources of the family — not just financial but also emotional and relational resources — are enhanced, not squandered?

These are serious questions, ones we are pleased to address in the pages of this book, based on our:

> » In-depth research into why so few family businesses
>   survive beyond the second generation
> » In-depth experience in helping family businesses plan and
>   implement succession policies and procedures, through the
>   Family Business Counsel of Canada (FBCC)

We have seen from our work that most family businesses lack the ability, strategic resources, and time necessary to put a successful succession plan into place on their own, and, more specifically, to communicate, implement, and maintain that plan. The Family Business Counsel of Canada helps family businesses deal with just such questions. We collaborate with professionals — including bankers, insurers, lawyers, and accountants — on an as needed basis to deal with specific issues faced by the family businesses that seek our help. And we monitor the progress of those businesses, assisting them in adapting their plan as conditions change.

Note that throughout this book we refer to The Succession Paradigm™.* This is the Family Business Counsel of Canada's proprietary and highly logical and effective succession planning process for family businesses. While the book you have in your hand is *an overview* of this succession planning approach, The Succession Paradigm itself is the *on-the-ground process* used to help companies navigate through the often complex and bewildering details of succession planning.

Succession planning is designed for those who want to create a legacy for future generations, whether that means operating the business and its proceeds more effectively or selling the business. The benefits of succession planning should be readily apparent. For example, a family business can substantially increase its value by saving on taxes through proper structuring. Furthermore, the family and family business can reduce legal costs because their lawyers have the benefit of advice from professional experts in the field.

Please allow us a few words of introduction about ourselves.

---

* More information about The Succession Paradigm™ is available through www.familybcc.com

» **Michael A. Lobraico,** president of the Family Business Counsel of Canada, is the force behind this book. As he relates in his story in the first chapter of this book, he experienced, as part of his family's transportation business, the painful strains to relationships that are inevitable when communication is poor within and between the three circles of a family business: the family, ownership, and business. He has turned this experience into a passion to help family businesses understand the importance of succession planning and communication. As part of his personal and professional mission, he has been active in the Canadian Association of Family Enterprises, including as its national president. He is a trained facilitator, executive coach, and mediator.

» **Jonathan Isaacs** has spent nearly three decades in the life insurance industry and specializes in the use of insurance as a tax planning tool. He, too, is part of a family that experienced loss because of poor succession planning. His great-grandfather, Sam Perilly, owned a flourishing cigarette manufacturing business, Perilly's Tobacco, in Kimberley, South Africa, in the late 1800s. Because of family conflict and sibling rivalry at the time of Perilly's passing, the firm was sold, for the grand sum of £20,000. Sam's company today is part of the multi-billion-dollar Rembrandt Group, which is owned by the Rupert Family in South Africa. Leaving business succession planning to chance caused significant loss for future generations of the Perilly family.

» **Mitchell Singer** is a lawyer with experience and expertise
   in tax and estate planning and life insurance planning.
   He brought his lawyer's eye, memory, and insight to bear
   on the writing of this book, particularly with regard to
   the "From a Legal Perspective" sections that close each
   chapter. He was particularly helpful in indicating various
   legal and tax issues that family businesses need to consider
   during the succession planning process.

Note that we have avoided using country- or jurisdiction-specific
information in this book in order to make the concepts and processes
that we discuss applicable across the English-speaking world, and,
indeed, beyond.

ACKNOWLEDGMENTS

This book was written as a result of many years of experience and research in our respective spheres of expertise — family business management, insurance, and law. We especially want to thank our colleagues Stephen Toale and Barry Block for their input and ideas.

This book would have been a mammoth task had it not been for the guidance and support of Donald Bastian of BPS Books. We also want to thank Jack David, publisher of ECW Press, for introducing him to us. Don helped us sharpen our communication of the processes of succession planning — in particular the strategies and systems we have developed as the Family Business Counsel of Canada (FBCC) to help synchronize family businesses in planning for the future. He helped us make it crystal clear how key, to both corporate survival and family harmony, this planning can be.

We would also like to thank the families and companies, as well as professionals from a variety of fields and expertise, that we have worked with over the years, as well as to acknowledge any family that has the courage and foresight to work on these issues.

Last but not least, we offer our thanks to our own families, who have supported us and opened our eyes in so many ways. We all are where we are today as a result of their support.

INTRODUCTION

When most people think of businesses, they think of the multinational corporations that trade on Wall Street or Bay Street: the blue-chip megaliths that make the news — for good or ill — day by day, quarter by quarter, and year after year.

The glitz and glamour of these companies obscure an important fact about the world of business, however — that *the most common form of business structure is not the multinational corporation but the family business*. Family businesses large and small employ millions of people all over the world, generating a large proportion of the world's jobs and cultural and philanthropic endeavors. These businesses drive the world's economy and societies.

In one of its recent annual studies of family businesses around the world, PriceWaterhouseCoopers reports that "the proportion of registered companies that are family controlled ... ranges from more than 50 percent in the European Union (EU) to between 65 percent and 90 percent in Latin America and over 95 percent in the US."[*]

In many cases, these family businesses are actually more viable and profitable than larger corporations, even though the latter have a greater number of shareholders and directors.

Most financial researchers agree on these sobering facts about family businesses:

>> A whopping 83 percent of family businesses do not survive the third generation

>> More than one third admit to conflicts over their future strategy

>> One quarter of these businesses say they have quarreled about the competence of family members actively involved in the business, or about who should be allowed to work for the company and who should not

>> Fully 70 percent of family businesses have not adopted any succession planning procedures or defined criteria for resolving conflicts

This lack of planning is going to grow more serious as baby boomers — whether they own businesses or not — receive inheritances and plan their own estates in greater and greater numbers. Some experts say that the greatest transfer of wealth in history will occur over the next fifty years. At least $41 trillion will pass to the next generation by 2044, according to Paul G. Schervish, director of the Center on Wealth and Philanthropy at Boston College.[**] The coming passage

---

[*] You can explore PWC's findings by visiting www.pwc.com

[**] John J. Havens and Paul G. Schervish, "Millionaires and the Millennium: New Estimates of the Forthcoming Wealth Transfer and the Prospects for a Golden Age of Philanthropy," Boston College Center on Wealth and Philanthropy.

of wealth will be in the form of cash and proceeds of insurance policies, but most of all from the transfer of assets in the form of property.

Many family businesses must address some big issues if they are to survive to the next generation, and soon. Succession planning should be high on their list of priorities. The reason is very simple. Corporate raiders and private equity firms will take advantage of this lack of planning to drive down the purchase price of family businesses, destroying the wealth of the families involved.

It is often assumed by family businesses that the corporate lawyer or accountant will be there to pick up the pieces. However, if these professionals were so competent, they would have attended to this most important planning process long before it became a concern. These professionals all too often overlook succession simply because it may not be high on their agendas or even close to their areas of expertise. This is the tough part of the process. It's important to start these conversations early to make sure that the planning happens.

• • •

What is succession planning? Succession planning is a multidisciplinary process that seeks to strategically structure an orderly transition of a company's management and ownership. A comprehensive approach focuses not only on traditional estate-planning concepts, but on many other important areas as well.

Given the sensitivities of family businesses and the threatening issues that can arise during succession planning, it is not surprising that many business owners attempt to avoid it altogether. The process has all the ingredients of a recipe for acrimony. It is both an individual business problem and a family problem where a parent or parents must assess the age, ability, maturity, desire, and personality of the children relative to the size and complexity of the business. When there are several or many children, both active and not active in the business, the problems increase in scope and intensity and can give way to sibling rivalry and conflict.

The plan developed with a family business ensures that the best decisions are made by and for the family, the owners, and the business. Fortunate indeed is the family business with a carefully considered and structured plan supported by family business succession advisors from various professions.

This book shows family businesses how to coordinate ideas and strategies into a logical sequence. As we have seen many times over, businesses that do follow this sequence of succession planning produce remarkable results. And not just financial results but emotional ones, as well. The good news is that succession planning can protect the three parts of any family businesses: the family, the business itself, and the owners. (Ownership is not necessarily held entirely by the family.)

Succession planning should be a top priority for all family businesses, both the big multinational ones like Four Seasons, S.C. Johnson, Wal-Mart, and Marriott, to name a few, and the small ones like the Smith family of Blooms Floral, the composite family business you will get to know in the second part of this book. As a result of the pace of technological change and the growing complexity of the economy, the leaders of family businesses, not just the leaders of GM, need to support and assist their CEO with the process of succession planning. A family business should always be ready for the unexpected with regard to succession. Always!

Even companies that have performed some aspects of succession planning quite often need to review their plans. Succession planning is an ongoing process. It is not a notebook to shelve until needed.

We do not pretend, in this book, to take you by the hand and show you exactly how to create and implement a succession plan. The variables from business to business are too great for them to be captured in any book of a reasonable size. Our purpose, rather, is to help you see the need for succession planning in your family business, grasp the essentials of how the process works, and begin the process yourself, turning to professionals for help as needed.

Here's a quick preview of what you'll be reading:

» The first part of this book shows you why family businesses need a succession plan, which may be thought of as a "corporate will"

» The second part takes you on the journey of one business — Blooms Floral, owned by the Smith family — through the five phases of the succession planning process. Seeing how this family business worked through the process will decrease your anxiety about succession planning. The knowledge you gain will definitely give you a better starting point

The good news is that you don't have to do this alone. It's possible, and advisable, for you to get help with this challenging yet ultimately liberating task by turning to outside advisors. A team approach to succession planning, such as that used by the Family Business Counsel of Canada, brings in and coordinates outside experts when and as needed.

PART 1

WHY YOU NEED
A CORPORATE WILL

CHAPTER 1

FAMILY BUSINESSES: A CAUTIONARY TALE

Most of you reading this book know how important it is to plan your estate and draw up a will: a legal document that directs how the assets of your estate are to be handled after you pass on. Most of you are well aware of the disasters that await the families of a parent who dies without a will. It can look like this:

» The court steps in to freeze the estate and decide how it is to be handled
» The family fights the court for the right to control the estate
» Family members fight each other for their piece of the pie (and the pie shrinks by the day as legal fees mount)
» The family and the business are changed forever

You can probably see where we're going with this. Yes, business owners need to understand the very similar importance of a will for their *corporation*:

> » A plan that mandates an orderly process for everyone concerned should they be incapacitated or wish to put the company in other hands or sell it outright
> » A plan to ensure that their intent and their wishes for their company and their family live on from generation to generation

Business owners without a corporate will put, in harm's way, the company they worked so hard and lovingly to build. Worse, they endanger the *family* part of their business. They are in danger of leaving a tragic *emotional* legacy behind them when they die.

It doesn't have to be this way. All parties involved in family business can get together on their intent for the family and the business. They can create and implement a succession plan that supports this intent and protects both riches and relationships.

To underscore the importance of an orderly succession planning process, the rest of this chapter is devoted to Michael A. Lobraico's story: a story that shows what can happen to a family as a result of poor communication about succession planning.

• • •

The story I'm about to tell you is written from my perspective. There are several other versions — whether those of my father, my brothers, or others. I'm telling my version in the hope that it will inspire other families to start the process of strengthening their communication within their family and their businesses. I truly believe that all family businesses have as their founding principle the intention of supporting the family unit. Sometimes this noble intent gets lost as the family, ownership, and business circles become blurred.

I am a member of the third generation of the family associated with the company OK Transportation Limited. This company was founded in Toronto in 1919 by my grandfather, Peter A. Lobraico, as OK Express. Subsequently it was led by my father, Vincent, who sold it to my brother, Peter A. Lobraico. He in turn sold it to another business in 2007. The company is no longer in family hands.

The company's origins and early years are fondly remembered in family lore, beginning with how the company got its name. Grandfather purchased a used truck emblazoned with the name O'Keefe Express. He scraped part of the name off its side, leaving "OK" as his company name. He couldn't afford to give his own name to his new enterprise, as others like the Buckley and Hendrie families were doing around that same time. He was a true entrepreneur, doing whatever it took to survive.

The early decades of the company feature Peter and his sons Michael and Vincent growing the business. This includes tales of how the three men dragged harps in trunks and other musical instruments up the wooden fire escape of the CBC building on Jarvis Street in Toronto, as well as delivering instruments to other studios on McGill and Grenville Streets; drove a truck up and down slippery Toronto streets as Michael and Vincent shoveled sand out the back onto snowy streets; heated the cabs of the trucks with bricks from the fireplace; filled their stomachs with tomato soup lunches made with ketchup and hot water; and purchased the company's first facility for $5,500 (heating it with wood burned in a forty-five-gallon drum).

Early on, the company committed itself to community service.

Over the years it supported local organizations and sports teams. It participated in national fundraising programs. My father and brother were the face of OK Transportation at the Rotary Club and the local hospital, where both of them sat on the board. As part of the family's ongoing community involvement, the Lobraico family honored the memory of my grandfather through the Lobraico Cardiac Rehabilitation Centre at the Rouge Valley Health Centre at the eastern edge of Toronto, Canada, which opened in 1997.

The company moved from strength to strength from its beginnings in 1919 right up to the turn of the new century. Michael and Vincent started working in the company in 1939, with their newly earned driver's licenses in hand. That was also the year that Canadian Westinghouse became OK's major customer.

Vincent (my father) became OK Transportation's second president, in 1952. He was passionately committed to customer service and expanded the company's routes, first to the rest of Ontario and then across the country. His and Peter's work ethic became the catalyst of the company's growth.

The rosy memories and the straight facts related above don't tell the full story, however. Although the business prospered, it did so in the face of poor communication within the family. So many important topics simply weren't talked about. Why? Because we did not make proper succession planning decisions. We did not have a basis for open conversations. Some important issues were swept under the carpet. We lacked a way to separate the issues and relationships involved in the family, ownership, and business circles of the family business.

My grandfather's intent was good and he was doing the best he could. In fact, he was determined to protect the family from the problems associated with a company's transition from one generation to the next. But he did so, unfortunately, by avoidance. He thought the best approach to choosing a successor was not to choose *one*. He stipulated that to own the company, his two sons, Michael and Vincent, would have to be 50-50 partners. He held 100 percent of the shares and sold them 50-50 to his sons. After this, he continued to help the company by taking care of various tasks — the daily banking, for example.

Upon his death in October 1979, family dynamics went into full swing. Communication between my grandfather and his children had been poor when it came to operating the business. He never informed the family of the details of generational transfer. His daughters were not involved in the business — Michael and Vincent's own daughters would end up doing odd jobs in the business, part time, as they grew up, but in our family, in keeping with attitudes of the times, it was considered inappropriate for women to work in a transportation business. Unfortunately, the daughters of the founder assumed that he would leave them money based on his ownership of the company. They weren't aware of the company's debt and leveraged position. This led to incorrect assumptions in the family, an all-too-common occurrence in family businesses.

The next transition involved Vincent's purchase of his brother Michael's shares. The details were not shared with the family. As I understand it, however, Vincent (my father) wanted to grow the business, which meant taking financial risks. Michael was happy with the company as it was. He decided to sell his portion of the business to avoid that risk. (Having five daughters may have contributed to his decision to sell his shares; as mentioned, in the tradition of our larger family, daughters were not to become leaders in the company or industry.) The brothers stayed close, but lack of communication about this transaction created a sense of unease among the members of the next generation.

During the ensuing years, many members of the third generation — Vincent's three sons and three daughters and Michael's five daughters — worked in the family business. Summer jobs were available to all.

Beginning in the late 1970s, Vincent's three sons — Peter, the eldest; John, the middle brother; and I, the youngest — joined the company.

Our father ran the company but gradually began to place more and more authority on Peter's shoulders. Father had lived through two poorly managed successions. He was aware of the strain caused by poor planning and miscommunication. He decided to create an effective succession plan. However, as was the style and expectation of the times, the plan glossed over the issue of Vincent's intent for the company. Furthermore, it was developed and executed by outside advisors — lawyers and accountants. The planning process certainly did not include discussions with John and me. The company's intent and the structures that supported that intent, including ongoing communication, were simply absent from the process.

In 1976, Vincent appointed Peter as the third president of OK Transportation. He sold him 20 percent of the shares of the company and continued working with him to grow the business. As in most transactions in family businesses, these shares were financed through the business.

That same year, John graduated from university and entered the company. He moved up the ranks over the next several years to become Vice President of Operations.

In 1984, I graduated from high school and moved to Fergus, Ontario, to work in a car dealership owned by the family. After two years I moved back to Toronto to drive a truck for the transportation company. I worked my way up to VP of Sales, responsible for customer relations and employee relations.

Because of poor — almost non-existent — succession planning conversations, John felt he had no option but to resign from the company. This happened in 2004. As I will describe in more detail below, I, too, withdrew from the company, a year later.

And in 2007, 88 years after the it was founded, Peter exercised his right to sell the company.

What happened?

Vincent and Peter communicated well with each other but not with John and/or me and the rest of the family. Father and eldest son did not know how to bring others into the succession planning conversation. Or perhaps they didn't want to. They were not clear about their expectations for the company. They lacked or did not share detailed plans regarding individual and corporate growth and development.

Don't get me wrong. As a family, and as leaders, we worked well together in the day-to-day running of the business. We made changes as conditions required and steadily grew the company. However, we failed to address some important questions, including:

» How the business should deal with the family
» What structures were needed for the ongoing success of the family and the business
» How the issues pertaining to ownership, family, and business should be separated and discussed

As for John and me, we were left on our own to speculate on the value we were contributing to the business and what our future paths might be.

My belief is that the disharmony that exists in our family to this day reflects not so much *what* happened as *how* it happened. There was a serious lack of conversation within the family about the company's business and relational concerns, ideas, and dreams for the present and the future. As a result, family members were not able to decide their own future within or outside the company based on the facts.

OK Transportation lacked governance rules defining what it meant to be a family member within the company. We knew we were different from regular employees but didn't know what that meant.

I can say from first-hand experience that the company played a large role in our family. We were very proud of our father and what he had created. He spent a great deal of time at work and the financial success that resulted enabled us to enjoy numerous family vacations and private school educations.

Perhaps because of my father's absence during my childhood, while he was building the company to support and feed us, one of the things I liked best about working in the company was the daily contact I had with him. I lost that when our working relationship became strained and meetings with lawyers and negotiators took the place of our daily conversations.

Knowing what I know now, I can see that two key rules for the success of a family business were broken right from the beginning.

First, no one had a clear plan with regard to the conditions for entering or exiting the company. There were no stipulations about the type of education we should get first or the development process once we entered the business. We didn't know what our annual performance expectations were or where we ranked as workers in the business and as partial owners of the business.

Second, there was no established process for each of us to communicate with the family in these three critical ways:

» As an employee seeking help or guidance
» As a sibling needing personal advice

» As a potential owner in terms of understanding the responsibilities of senior leadership and ownership

Meetings that *did* deal with ownership and succession issues were unplanned and sporadic. They lacked a clear purpose. I was not able to ask questions regarding ownership. Any conversations that did take place were one-way: from the top down. I was led to believe, on the basis of sketchy communication, that I would eventually be brought into ownership. "Some day this all will be clear" was the prevailing sentiment. (Not unlike what owners of family businesses often say to their children: "Some day, all this will be yours.")

By the turn of the century, I was married with a growing family. I wanted to play a larger role within the company. Given my traditional upbringing, I sought to be my family's sole provider through the family business. I lacked the confidence — and an invitation — to ask any questions about ownership that might rock the boat. My future was in other people's hands.

Furthermore, I was worried about my employability *outside* the business. After all, my formal education ended when I graduated from high school and I had never worked outside the family business, a common situation for family members working in their family's business.

At some point in the early years of the present century the conversation about ownership was opened up to John and me. It wasn't really a conversation, though. We were informed of the ownership structure. We were given some shares in the company. It was made clear that there would be only one majority shareowner: Peter, the eldest son. The shares were not divided equally between my middle brother and me. This was not discussed and the process was not open to negotiation or collaboration. John and I were also briefly walked through the company shareholder agreement.

These conversations took place near the end of the legal process. We were not privy to discussions about the premise, purpose, and implementation of these decisions.

At the time I did not realize that I should protect myself with separate legal counsel. I just signed the agreement. I thought this was the way these things were done in a family enterprise. I was happy to be formally recognized as an owner.

John and I were invited to board meetings, but the power in the family and the business remained with Peter and my father.

Over the next several years, John and I bought the preferred shares from them. The price the company paid for these shares came into conversation several times during those years. To the best of my recollection, no regular dividends were paid on the common shares owned by the three of us.

As John and my contributions and responsibilities grew in the company, so did our questions regarding compensation, the perks of ownership, and most importantly how we could have input into the future of the company. What would our roles look like in five, ten, or even fifteen years? We simply didn't know.

Friction between my two older brothers continued to increase. From what I could see, John's vision of how the company should grow involved taking strategic risks. Peter's vision was conservative. He wasn't prepared to change a model that had served him and the company well.

After several years, on the basis of private conversations with advisors but very few open ones as a group or as separate family, ownership, and business circles, Peter decided that things needed to change and that my middle brother should leave the company.

I was told about his departure after the decision had been made. That conversation was window-dressing. In retrospect, I regret that I did not speak up. Was my failure to do so caused by fear, ignorance, or greed — or a combination of all three? I'm not sure. In the end, John was out of the company and I purchased his shares.

John's departure sparked a serious deterioration of family relationships, although fortunately John and I have remained close in spite of these events. I was — and am — grateful for the lessons he taught me.

After John left, there were two owners of our company: Peter, who had the majority of the shares and continued acting independently, and me, with fewer shares and lots of questions and ideas. I wanted to know the rules of the game, including:

» What we could expect from each other
» How we could share responsibility for growing
  the company
» What the plan was for bringing the fourth generation
  of Lobraicos into the business

To this day I believe my questions were misunderstood, and I take some of the responsibility for that. Again, these conversations were doomed because there was no succession planning structure to support — let alone encourage — them.

Tensions grew between Peter and me. The conversations we should have been having with each other morphed into conversations between his lawyers and advisors and mine.

Things came to a head when I was asked to attend an offsite meeting with my father and a family friend/advisor. Peter would not be in attendance. I was given very few details about what was to be on the agenda. Sensing from my father's tone of voice that something was up, I asked a lawyer and other business family mentors for advice on my options based on the various scenarios that might come into play in the meeting.

We began the meeting with some light conversation. Then the advisor turned to me.

"We would like to do this without lawyers," he said, passing me an envelope.

I refused to open it.

There was some further discussion as they encouraged me to open the envelope. My father said he was there to help.

I could tell he meant well and said to him, "It's not fair for us to put you in the middle and have you pick between your sons."

What I didn't realize was that my father had already chosen.

I had spoken to my father almost daily for more than twenty years as a friend, a mentor, and a trusted advisor. Now the relationship was changed, forever. During negotiations and for several years following, we would speak only a few times. I miss the conversations and the closeness we once had.

I don't want to go into the details of the ensuing events because that would be unfair to my father, my brothers, sisters, my wife and children, and me. However, I do believe it would help you to know some key points.

After I tried several ways to improve my negotiation position, my wife and I decided to settle with the business out of court. The emotional and financial pressure was too hard to bear.

I thought my brother and I would sign the deal and be cordial to each other, perhaps even shaking hands. I was surprised and disappointed when my lawyer informed me that the deal would have a "non participatory closing" — Peter would not attend. As things turned out, I wouldn't see or speak to my brother for more than two years. During that time his son was married and he became a grandfather.

Since then, other than at Christmas functions and some family events, there has been no real connection between my brother and me, despite various attempts to mend what was broken in our family during this difficult period.

In closing my story, let me ask you something. Have you ever heard the saying, "There are no friends in business"? Of course this is not always true, but the saying makes a very important point. The rules that apply when people make business decisions often threaten the bonds of friendship. Business dealings can hurt a friendship, and friendship can compromise business dealings.

The same is true when it comes to family businesses: "There are no family members in business." Here's what happens all too often:

>> Family members involved in a business tend to ignore questions about the purpose of their business because they're family

>> They tend to avoid building and following strong business processes because they're family.

>> They avoid discussing controversial decisions because they're family

Families expect goodwill and family loyalty to carry the day. However, businesses are about profits and families are about feelings. If families don't separate the two and agree to work together under the guidance of strong business processes and decisions, both the profits of the business and the feelings of the family will suffer. When family businesses run themselves like proper businesses, they can actually become stronger businesses *and* families.

And it's proper succession planning that makes all the difference, as you will see in the rest of this book.

FROM A LEGAL PERSPECTIVE

A corporate will is an important document that ensures that the wishes of the owner(s) of the business are carried out. Although technically it is not a legal document, one patriarch took things to an extreme to give legal effect to a corporate will while saving significant probate taxes.

The use of multiple wills in Ontario (Canada) was first recognized and accepted by the courts in *Granovsky Estate v. Ontario*. In that case, the testator, Philip Granovsky, died leaving two wills.

The "primary will" dealt with all of his property except for shares in the capital of certain private corporations, amounts receivable from the private corporations, and assets held in trust for Mr. Granovsky by the private corporations.

The assets excluded from the primary will totaling nearly $25 million were dealt with under a "secondary will." A limited grant of probate of the primary will was issued by the court on the condition that the executors bring an application before the court to determine the status of the two wills. Probate fees were paid on the value of the assets governed by the primary will. The secondary will was not submitted to probate, nor were any probate fees paid on the value of the assets governed by that will.

Effectively, what Mr. Granovsky's estate did was avoid paying probate on his biggest asset: his interest in the family business, Atlantic Packaging. The theory was simple. Mr. Granovsky kept his family informed about the contents of his will, and by formalizing those intents ensured that probate was not needed. No one contested the secondary will because everyone knew its contents ahead of time.

Although this type of dual will planning may not exist in every jurisdiction, this case demonstrates that keeping the family informed ensures a smoother succession. Even if a family proves to be unsuccessful in saving the probate fees on the secondary will, this type of planning will make the transfer of the business to the next generation more harmonious.

CHAPTER 2

HOW SUCCESSION PLANNING WORKS: AN OVERVIEW

Consider the following scene — one that is unfortunately all too common in family businesses.

• • •

The hallways of the head office of ABC Widgets Company were abuzz with activity. When employees arrived that morning, they learned that an emergency meeting had been called for 11:30 a.m. Speculation was rampant. Nervous employees spoke in whispers around water coolers.

Robert Jones Jr., the owner and president of the company, had been away from the office for some time. It was a poorly kept secret that he had been seriously ill. Jones was universally loved by his staff. He had a warm smile and a friendly greeting for everyone in his

HOW SUCCESSION PLANNING WORKS: AN OVERVIEW

employ, from senior VPs to line workers. He genuinely cared about all of his employees, and they responded with fierce loyalty and unflagging enthusiasm. His absence had been deeply felt.

Information Technology staff were busy in the cavernous boardroom preparing equipment to broadcast the meeting to ABC Widget branch offices around the world. Not since the death of Jones's father and predecessor ten years earlier had a general meeting been convened so abruptly and with such anxiety.

By 11:30 the boardroom had filled to capacity. Those who arrived late stood at the great oak doors or remained at their desks and cubicles where they would watch the webcast. The vast room was impossibly silent as Peter Goldman, the company's veteran CFO and the Jones family's close friend, stepped to the podium.

"Ladies and gentlemen," he began. "I regret to inform you that Robert Jones Jr., our beloved president and owner, died yesterday of a heart attack ..."

In the midst of their sadness and shock over losing their leader, individuals in the boardroom couldn't help but think about what would happen next.

» Shareholders wondered whether an interim CEO would be able to hold everything together; whether their shareholder value would be safe; and whether the contingencies the company had in place would be strong enough to get it through choppy waters

» Senior executives were concerned about whether they were in the running to be the next CEO

» Managers and staff wondered whether their job was secure

» Members of the ownership family wondered whether they

would be called on to help with succession matters. Would the company remain strong enough to pay the yearly dividend?

Other issues complicated the matter considerably. Dick Jones, Bob's brother, was a major shareholder of the firm but not a working executive. He enjoyed the privileges that came from being a Jones, including the directors' remuneration allotted to him and the recognition he attracted because of who he was. Would he jockey for position in the company — perhaps even as the interim CEO — to protect his future earnings?

Meanwhile, no one was sure of the reactions of members from one power family in the Jones connection who held down various management positions. Those positions had been given to them because of family connections, not because of their education before entering the firm or their development thereafter.

This had caused morale problems among employees who are ripe to become middle managers. After all, the career ladder is so much harder to climb when various rungs are reserved for people with a certain last name.

ABC Widgets was headed for disaster because it wasn't set up as a business to survive sudden change in leadership. The Jones family itself was headed for disaster, too, because structures were not in place to help them separate business issues from family issues.

• • •

Many family businesses need assistance in situations like this. The Succession Paradigm process, as described below (pages 27–34), helps

family businesses prepare for transition, keeping the family, ownership, and business strong and growing.

THE SUCCESSION PARADIGM PROCESS

The rest of this chapter deals in broad strokes with the five phases of
the Succession Paradigm Process. This overview will prepare you for
the second part of this book, which is composed of chapters on these
phases, using a composite business, Blooms Floral, as an extended
case study for illustrative purposes.

The following diagram gives you an overview of our Succession
Paradigm approach to succession planning.

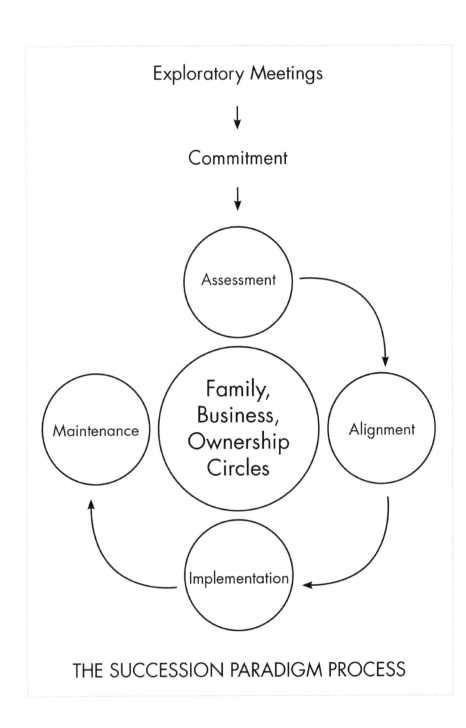

Exploratory Meetings

Commitment

Assessment

Family,
Business,
Ownership
Circles

Maintenance

Alignment

Implementation

THE SUCCESSION PARADIGM PROCESS

PHASE 1 / INTRODUCTION

We usually start by meeting with the company or family's senior leadership to ensure that they and we understand the overarching needs of their company with respect to succession planning. The premise is that the business needs to be strong and stable in order to support this planning process.

We then send the company a formal pre-engagement letter as an opening communication with the family, ownership, and senior leadership. This letter confirms the succession planning process and its complexities as outlined in some detail in our previous meeting.

Next, we hold a meeting with the owners and leaders. We need to introduce ourselves to them, and they need to introduce themselves to us. We describe the process we'll be going through together. We stress that it is premature at this point to get into the details of the process — the *how* of succession planning. We discuss the purpose of the process with them first — the *why* of the business, the family, and the ownership.

Specifically, we want to understand the owners' intent for the business. What is its purpose? Is it to provide jobs and salaries to family members, whether they are qualified or not? To provide opportunities to them only if they complete a specific development plan? Or do the owners see the company as an investment that is best left in the hands of non-family professionals?

The introductory phase often helps the family, owners, and senior business leaders to clarify and agree on the purpose of the business as a business per se and vis-à-vis the family.

PHASE 2 / ASSESSMENT

In the assessment phase we compare the agreements and vision that have emerged during the first phase against the organizational structure of the company: Who is in what positions? Who reports to whom? Which workers are family and which are non-family? Who are the senior leaders? Who are the junior leaders? The middle management? The employees? Does everyone know where they fit and what their roles are?

We assess the company's shareholder agreement, its organizational structures, and its in-house and outside advisors. We are thus enabled to start asking these important questions:

> » What are the goals of the family, ownership, and the business?
> » What structures are in place to support these goals?
> » Are the right people in the right jobs?
> » Are the junior leaders on track to become senior leaders?
> » What is the financial strength of the company, in terms of how it is organized, the type of business it is, and how it measures up to the competition?

The assessment phase also involves projection: What is expected for the company over the next year, the next three to five years, and beyond? Based on the ages of the senior leaders, when are succession issues likely to arise? What effect might their retirement, for example, have on future earnings?

Using our Succession Paradigm process, we evaluate the company's existing strategies against best-practice alternative processes to identify any antiquated programs and general inefficiencies.

PHASE 3 / ALIGNMENT

At this point, the assessment process moves into the alignment phase, which includes the formation of the succession plan for the family, ownership, and the business.

This phase involves identifying talent in the company, as well as the company's capabilities and effectiveness. Is the company tapping into its talent? Are its capabilities being used effectively? What we report back to leadership at this point can be a bitter pill for them to swallow. This is when we test our ideas mid-course to see whether we're on the right track, and, more importantly, to gauge how much buy-in we have from leadership. Are the correct structures and people in place for ongoing growth and success?

By this point we have a good grasp of the company and its purposes, people, and performance. We are able now to create the actual plan and present it to the owners and senior leaders. The plan puts into writing:

» The ongoing vision of the company
» The organizational structure
» The roles and responsibilities attached to the positions defined by that structure
» The process that will be followed when senior and family positions change due to growth needs, retirement, illness, or death

PHASE 4 / IMPLEMENTATION

Presenting the plan to the leaders almost always brings about changes and fine tuning. We welcome this because it means leadership is fully engaged in the process.

Once the plan has been revised, we are ready to work with the company to support it during implementation.

At this point, the plan needs to be carefully analyzed and revised by the company's in-house financial leader and the company's lawyer, when and where needed. For example, because it may not speak to the situation of the company, the company's shareholder agreement may need to be revised. In about 60 percent of the cases we deal with, a whole new agreement must be drawn up. Either way, the formal agreement of a majority of the shareholders is required to make these changes.

This implementation phase is key. However well developed a succession plan is, putting it into action can prove difficult given that all those involved are immersed in their day-to-day jobs.

PHASE 5 / MAINTENANCE

In most cases, the Family Business Counsel of Canada's involvement with the company is a long-term one. Besides going through the phases described above, we also help through an ongoing maintenance phase. We review the succession plan on a regular basis, making sure that processes are under way and targets reached as the plan specifies. Yearly reviews ensure that goals, strategies, policies, and legal documents are aligned and are assisting the company — family, ownership, and business — in working toward succession planning goals.

Many approaches to succession planning are theoretical, leaving company leaders scratching their heads regarding how they should be applied to the practical needs of the business.

Other plans are simply a list of procedures. They are, for all intents and purposes, a series of chronological do's and don'ts. Since reality rarely cooperates with these lists, internal management ends up making too many exceptions and the plan soon degenerates into arbitrary decision making.

In contrast, the Succession Paradigm approach:

» Is a dynamic process, which means it is more comprehensive. It addresses a wider range of actual and potential issues. It deals with some of the most intricate problems that a CEO can face during succession planning

» Is a collaborative process, bringing all key internal and external players together to create the strategy needed for succession

» Adopts a long-term approach for sustainability of the owners' wealth

» Identifies the central questions that must be addressed, and results in a method to implement change coordinated with the support of the Family Business Counsel of Canada, under the leadership of a strong facilitator

» Puts in place a qualified facilitator to coordinate each session with the family, the owners, and the business leaders. These sessions are explained in the initial interview and take place at prescribed intervals. Throughout the process, meetings are facilitated with management, advisors, and shareholders and meetings are held with key members individually. Information is collated, coordinated, and integrated into the plan

» Deals with issues that are fundamental to the owners, including intergenerational wealth transfer, estate freeze opportunities, retirement compensation arrangements, family trusts, charitable foundations, wills, buy-sell agreements, and income-tax minimization and deferral

» Assists the family business owner in the preparation and gathering of information necessary to make informed decisions regarding the future of the family business. The SP approach is not to be viewed as a replacement tool for using professional advisors, but as a tool that will enhance the process. The Family Business Counsel of Canada welcomes the input and support of a family company's professional advisors. These advisors become an integral part of the team. The legal, financial, and taxation implications of succession planning can be enormous. Professional advisors are worked with in a collaborative manner

» Puts in place a code of ethics, a confidentiality agreement, and privacy statements. We expect the family to read the full versions of these documents and sign off on all of them. Information and data are carefully guarded. Our findings and reports also fall under the disclosure statements mentioned above

In summary, family businesses need a corporate will that expresses the intent of the owner for the business, and a succession plan that protects all three circles of the family business: family, ownership, and business.

FROM A LEGAL PERSPECTIVE

At the end of the book, you will see a list of documents that your lawyers may need to create or alter in order to ensure a smooth succession plan (see Appendix 1). Although it is not an exhaustive list, it will help you see that the number of documents your lawyer, or lawyers, must understand to successfully implement a family succession plan is immense.

There are some important considerations in choosing a lawyer. First and foremost, you must choose one with the right expertise. Just as you wouldn't ask your family physician to be your cardiac surgeon, so you shouldn't expect your real estate lawyer to handle complicated succession planning issues. You don't choose a lawyer just because he or she went to law school. Law school is a place to learn about the law, but it's not where lawyers are made. Lawyers are made in practice through experience. You need to make sure you have a lawyer with expertise and experience in succession planning, will planning, and corporate transactions. If your lawyer is not an expert in these areas, let him or her employ a colleague who can give you the expertise you need.

Another important criterion is whether the lawyer is easy to get along with. It's possible that people from all three circles (family, ownership, and business) will be dealing with this lawyer and other legal professionals. If the lawyer creates an adversarial environment, it may carry over into business or family functions. Look for a lawyer who embraces planning and who wants to create a warm environment for family dealings. Finding the right lawyer is key. If you search, you will find the one who is right for you.

You should get your lawyer involved early on. You will need to understand early in the succession planning process what constraints of any legal entities and planning may have been put in place prior to this process. By getting the lawyer involved early, you will save money in the long run. Your lawyer will help you avoid bad ideas before they take on a life of their own. This not only will save money, it will also prevent strife.

PART 2

THE SUCCESSION PARADIGM PROCESS: THE BLOOMS FLORAL STORY

CHAPTER 3

THE THREE CIRCLES OF
A FAMILY BUSINESS

In the first part of this book we helped you become more aware of
two factors that are essential to the success of a family business:

» First, everyone involved needs to be open and clear — as
   family, owners, and business leaders — in all of their
   conversations and dealings
» Second, a succession plan, which we described as a
   corporate will, must be developed and maintained

These two factors are intimately connected because a succession
plan, when properly set up and maintained, is in fact the mechanism
that actually *creates* openness in a family business. When, through a
succession plan, the goals, structures, and processes of ownership and
the business are out in plain sight for all to see, there are fewer miscon-
ceived assumptions and expectations in the family and the business.

This means there are fewer disappointments and fewer recriminations. (Unfortunately, these negative experiences are occupational hazards of a family business. But it doesn't have to be this way.)

This part of our book is devoted to showing you how the Family Business Counsel of Canada helps family businesses develop this kind of openness by creating a plan that takes into account all of the realities of the family, ownership, and the business. Although your business may be very different from the composite one we will describe — Blooms Floral — seeing the process for yourself will help you understand your own situation better. It will help you to begin, or revise, your succession plan.

Before we move into the individual chapters on the phases of succession planning, we'd like to give you a bird's-eye view of how you can begin to sort out the complexity of a family business. You may be anticipating what this sorting principle is. In our description of the five phases above, we repeatedly mentioned the *three circles of a family business*:

» The family
» The ownership
» The business

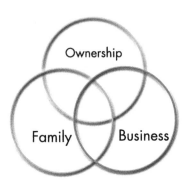

It's true that family businesses are not all alike. They range from one-member entrepreneurial efforts to large companies with hundreds if not thousands of workers, and from organizations that focus on a neighborhood, city, or region to those with multiple locations in several different countries. However, every family business *is* the same in one key respect: They are all made up of these three circles of family, ownership, and business.

We've seen it over and over again. People involved in a family business feel a sense of relief when they're helped to distinguish these three circles. Their hopes for understanding and clarity rise when we show them how we will work with those involved in each circle to clarify and communicate each circle's structures, processes, and goals. And they become engaged in the process when we paint a picture of how the three-circles approach will help them develop productive methods for communicating not only within each circle but also between circles.

In many cases, *not* seeing this tripartite reality of a family business is what keeps family businesses from even getting started on a succession plan. Their situation just seems too complex to them. And dangerous, too. For example:

» Family members may be anxious about whether they'll get their financial piece of the pie should the business be sold. Or worse, they may assume that they're in line for a windfall, unaware that the company is highly leveraged because it is in the midst of a five-year plan for growth

» Meanwhile, the owners of the company may fear the family pressures they'll face if senior management of the business tells a member of the family he or she is not ready for a senior management role in the company

» And rank-and-file workers in the business may fear being passed over for a promotion because they're not part of the family

Can you see the potential for miscommunication, misunderstanding, anxiety, and anger when structures and processes are not in place to deal with issues like these?

A Common Misconception

It is often thought that family members who are not acting or working in the business are not involved in or affected by three-circle issues. This is a mistake. Where there are non-active children, one must attempt to insure that all parties perceive that they are being dealt with in a fair, though not necessarily equal, manner. Dealing effectively with the issues of succession requires the business owner to view the process as a financial decision and not just a personal one.

A very special set of interactions will most likely take place between family, employees, and ownership groups (if applicable). Many of these groups overlap. For example, an inactive shareholder who wants a regular payment of dividends may have different goals and expectations concerning business decisions than active shareholders do. The latter may prefer investing profits back into the business. A careful analysis is needed to show the conflicts that are inherent in this situation. Only by planning and communication will these issues be resolved — and acrimony avoided.

IT'S A MATTER OF SURVIVAL

The reason family businesses so often spiral out of control is that both the family and the business are committed to their own survival, yet their survival goals and methods are so different.

> » A family is deeply committed to its own survival. "Blood is thicker than water" is one way to put it. Even in the strongest and most loving of families, family members are not able to be objective about their relationships. Why do you think it's an ethical and professional rule that doctors should not operate on members of their family and lawyers should not represent family members? Because a family's instinct to survive is so strong, individual family members find it difficult to make rational judgments when someone they are related to is threatened, whether emotionally, physically, or financially

> » A business, meanwhile, is also committed to survival. To survive, it must make a profit. It borrows money for the capital it needs to develop a product or service that it can sell at a price that is greater than costs and taxes. Otherwise it can't pay back its loan, meet its payroll, pay dividends to investors, and live to fight another day

An essential principle rises from this reality: *The key to succession planning is to set up structures and processes that keep these two types of survival from leveraging each other for survival.* Luke's ERROR

Here's an example of how a right intention in one circle can go wrong with respect to the other circles. Consider a family connected to the business that follows its survival instinct by getting the children a job in the family business. If these children lack the training or ability to do the job well, the family has hampered the business. The family's urge to help the next generation to survive is now threatening the business's ability to survive. The children or next generation are now a burden on the business because they are drawing a salary but doing little to increase profits. (And what about the children themselves? Their dreams for their future may not include working in the business. Bowing to family pressure doesn't help them, either.)

Similarly, if the business, when it is in dire straits financially, reaches out to ownership to bail it out with a loan or gift of money, it fails to make tough decisions and run itself on sound business principles.

Instead of learning from its difficulties and developing checks and balances to get it through similar rough times in the future, it has introduced into its very culture the un-businesslike notion that the family will always be there to prop the business up.

Here's another essential principle: *A good succession plan ensures that structures and processes are put in place and respected so that both the family and the business survive, without threatening each other's survival or the financial position of the owners.*

For example, a rule can be made that a family member will be considered for a job in the business only if he or she merits it based on company policies concerning entry into the company, including meeting certain educational and experience requirements. Rules can also make it clear to the business circle of a family business that the family is not a cash machine for the business to access when its planning or work is substandard or when it hits an economic trough.

Stated more positively, a good succession plan puts processes into place that enable the family, ownership, and the business to support each other in their desire to survive and thrive as family, owners, and business leaders and staff.

Now it's time to turn to the chapters on the five phases of succession planning.

FROM A LEGAL PERSPECTIVE

Although in the list at the end of the book (Appendix 1) we have separated legal documents into the documents that pertain to the three circles, you will notice some duplication from list to list. When documents are created, they have an influence on the different circles. Although the documentation needs may be unique for each circle, the documents from circle to circle will have a lot in common, too.

For example, on its face an employment contract to employ the president and CEO looks like a corporate document. But what happens when the president is the eldest daughter of the patriarch of the family? That document is personal to a family member now. Furthermore, if the company has a share purchase plan, how is ownership in the company affected? How does the situation just mentioned compare with that of the president's sister who chose to become a doctor and not be involved in the family business?

This example is meant to demonstrate the need for proper planning and consideration with respect to the circles and their influence on each other. All legal documentation should secure the family, the ownership, and the business without threatening any of them. All three should exist independently, but their influence on each other must never be forgotten.

CHAPTER 4

PHASE 1 / INTRODUCTION

Melissa Smith, a business owner in London, Ontario, called us a few years ago. She wanted to discuss whether we could help her sort out a complex family business crisis.* We were pleased to meet with her for an informal chat to understand her needs and get an overview of her business, her family, and the structure of the ownership of the business.

Melissa told us a compelling story in that meeting of a business that started small and grew into a thriving enterprise through several expansions across Canada and into the United States.

• • •

Eric Smith and Melissa Reynolds married in July 1960. Both were twenty years old. They had immigrated to Canada from Ireland with

---

* Names and details have been changed to protect the privacy of clients.

their respective families just after World War ll. Melissa and Eric grew up in Toronto, inheriting their parents' strong work ethic and entrepreneurial drive.

In September of that same year, the couple moved to London, Ontario, to build a life together. True to their upbringing, they believed the best way to build long-term wealth and security for their family was to start their own business. They decided to build on Melissa's gardening skills — which she had learned from her mother — by opening a floral shop.

Using their pooled savings from wedding gifts and gifts from their parents, they opened Blooms Floral, in 1961. Before long, their small shop had built an excellent reputation and the company began to find its financial footings.

Blooms wasn't the only thing that was growing. In three short years, from 1961 to 1963, Eric and Melissa were blessed with the arrival of their children Robert, Patricia, and Steven.

Blooms purchased two additional stores in 1962, one of them in Toronto and the other in Ottawa. Eric worked long hours running all three locations. The financial pressure was intense because the couple had decided to purchase each store location on their own instead of inviting other investors to join them. As a result, they were paying off large loans to several banks.

While Eric juggled the management of the stores, Melissa juggled administrative and creative oversight of the company and the challenges of a busy household. Both parents chipped in to help manage household chores, as needed.

The Smiths decided to stop at three children ... but not at three stores. They realized by now that further expansion of their business would require additional financial and managerial support. They opted to take on a business partner, Frank Lewis, a London-based entrepreneur. He purchased 15 percent of the company shares. The three owners went on to buy three new locations, a second one in Ottawa and two in Toronto. During the 1970s the company opened several stores in Ontario, British Columbia, and Quebec.

Expansion put pressure on all three owners. Melissa stuck close to home and the children, managing the three stores in London. Eric was on the road most days as he supervised the rest of the Ontario stores. Frank was away almost full-time, tending to the stores outside the province.

Because the ownership team was working so hard *in* the business, they neglected the all-important task of working *on* the business. They neglected to take the time to create structures, processes, and goals for the business. They failed to take a hard look, with the aid of their lawyer, at their shareholder agreement. Life was just moving too fast for anyone to stop and think about where the company was heading.

The Smiths' children started helping out part-time during the 1970s, and then joined the business full-time by the 1980s as they hit their young adult years.

As the company reached its thirtieth anniversary, in 1991, change was in the air. Frank was ready to slow down. He was tired of all the travel his role required. And he wanted to reduce his financial risk as he entered his retirement years.

Like most families who run their own business, Eric and Melissa, along with Frank, had plowed retained earnings back into the business to help fund its growth and security. The three owners agreed that Melissa and Eric would purchase 50 percent of Frank's 15 percent share in the company, leaving Frank with a 7.5 percent ownership position. They agreed that he would step down from his day-to-day responsibilities and segue to more of an advisory role.

His ownership position meant he would benefit from future profits realized by the business.

In the last decade of the century, the company was able to finish the purchase of the shares Frank had sold to it and establish its presence farther afield — in the northern United States. However, in 1998, while on a trip to the US, Eric suffered a serious heart attack. The family and business were not prepared for the pressures this caused. They had given little thought to how the business would operate if something happened to one of the owners, or, indeed, to other leaders in the business.

Eric's doctor told him to take a year off to convalesce, but Eric was back at work within a month. He felt he had to do what he could to help Melissa with the greater pressure she was facing as a result of his illness. Melissa, meanwhile, was torn between her increased business demands and her desire to spend more time with Eric to help him regain his health.

The company had hired Sheldon Feinstein as its Chief Financial Officer during the restructuring of shares and leadership roles with Frank's exit from day-to-day responsibilities. Now, with the family and company in turmoil, Melissa and Frank asked Sheldon to expand his responsibilities and manage the company.

By this time, the extended Smith family was thoroughly embedded in the business. Eric and Melissa's three children, Robert, Patricia, and Steve, were joined in the company by an in-law and several grandchildren, some of whom worked full-time and some part-time.

Unfortunately, Eric did not recover. He died of a second heart attack ten months after his first. A cloud of uncertainty hung over the company. Melissa's focus, as a result of Eric's death and her thoughts of retirement, was changing. She no longer felt as passionate about the business. She wanted to spend more time with her family — after all, caring for her family was why she and Eric started working in the business in the first place.

Melissa's change of focus caused others to start asking some important questions, such as:

» Who would lead Blooms Floral in the coming years?
» What structures were needed to support Eric and Melissa's original goals and dreams for the company and the family?
» What would ownership look like in the coming years?
» Did these goals still fit the business?
» And what about the senior management of the business? Would family members get the positions or promotions that came open because of their last name? Or would merit and experience be the criteria anyone, whether family or not, had to meet if they wanted to move into the corner offices?

What About You?

Have you thought about who will lead your company in the future? About your original and current intentions for the company? About the rules for the involvement, in the business, of your children or other relatives?

It was at this point that Melissa called the Family Business Counsel of Canada. She had heard about us and our work through another family business owner we had helped. She wanted us to guide her in navigating some upcoming conversations and decisions regarding the family and its values and legacy, on the one hand, and the future of the business, on the other. Melissa knew she couldn't manage this process on her own and have any reasonable hope of success. We at FBCC began our work with her in 1999 and have been advising her and other family members and senior executives ever since.

How We Are Called On to Help

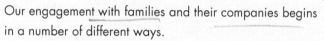

Our engagement with families and their companies begins in a number of different ways.

» Sometimes people approach us after hearing one of us make a presentation on succession planning and/or on other topics affecting family-owned and -operated companies

» Other times a business owner's trusted advisor — often a lawyer or an accountant — gets in touch with us and introduces us to their client

» We have also been called by senior non-family executives who are not necessarily involved in the ownership of the business but are concerned about the security of the business and want to introduce us to the company's owners

» Sometimes a member of the next generation of the family expresses concern about their parents or family in general or about management and the future of the business and brokers a meeting between us and the company's ownership

» Sometimes a progressive leader of a business that is in excellent shape wants to sort out family business issues while the children are still in school, before a crisis arises. The leader wants to create a clear communication process that separates the three circles and wants to know well in advance what the owners' position is on family members entering the business

Our aim is to get companies thinking about succession earlier — in advance of such challenges, rather than in the midst of them.

The situation with Melissa and her company was fairly common. Companies usually call us in because of a family or company crisis, such as a problem with the children, the ill health or death of an owner or senior leader, or a drop in demand for the company's products.

After the initial meeting, we sent Melissa a letter to underscore what we had said about the reason for, and importance of, succession planning. The letter confirmed our understanding of her and the company's situation and summarized our Succession Paradigm approach to succession planning.

GETTING THE BIG PICTURE

Although the shape and scope of the introductory phase of succession planning varies from company to company, how we proceeded with Melissa's company is fairly typical.

We requested a meeting with her, Frank, who still owned 7.5 percent of the company, and Sheldon Feinstein, the Chief Financial Officer. In that meeting we confirmed the membership of the Family Business Counsel of Canada succession planning team, indicating which individuals would work with them, and when, at different points in the process. (Some would be brought in, as needed, to work on very specific technical issues, such as tax law and insurance.)

We spoke in very broad terms about the three components of the family business — the family, ownership, and the business — to determine who should be present from each component in the next meeting — a larger introductory meeting.

In that larger meeting, held a month later, we focused on the range of complexities that surround family-owned businesses, particularly those that are entering the second or third generation. We discussed major factors in the high rate of family business failure, including the lack of effective succession planning and the lack of a sophisticated and comprehensive business model.

We pointed out that there are succession plans and there are succession plans and described how a family business sometimes fails in the second or third generation, despite having a traditional succession plan, because the plan is poorly communicated or not followed (put on a shelf) or is not specific to their family, or a combination of the above. The plan may fail to take into account the emotional and personal factors involved in family businesses. Further, it may not be comprehensive but be focused rather narrowly on the family unit; in fact, these plans are sometimes essentially an extension to a last will and testament.

Admittedly, this introductory meeting was tough. But there was no substitute for facing the facts about the lack of understanding that existed in this case about structure and the critical distinctions between family, ownership, and business. Everyone needed to face the fact that very little thought had gone into succession planning within any of the three circles while Eric, Melissa, and Frank were running and growing the business.

Sugar coating the situation would not have done anyone any favors. We weren't there to make everybody happy but to emphasize the need for honesty and clarity. We pointed out that each family business situation comes with different questions, different understandings and expectations, and different levels of openness to sharing information. We indicated that our goal was to get everyone working with the same information to create cohesive goals and outcomes.

We described how such discussions enable each person to choose for themselves what they wanted to do with their lives. We encouraged them to ask themselves, depending on where they fit in the three circles: Do I want to enter the business? Do I want to continue in the business? Do I want to be on my own? We added that everyone needed to understand the choices that were possible for them and what the consequences might look like for each decision. And that clarity on these issues could be achieved only when they learned to separate family from employment and ownership.

In summary, we went over:

- » The importance of succession planning
- » The process of succession planning
- » The three circles of a family business (and who the senior representatives of those circles were)
- » Who fit in each circle, both now and in the future. For example, Melissa was able to articulate that she was thinking of leaving the business circle because she no longer wished to run the company; this brought certain questions to light for her, such as, "Do I want to remain part of the ownership circle?"
- » How we would meet with each component separately and then together as we aligned the processes, structures, and goals of each circle with the others
- » The various options of a company like Blooms Floral — e.g., reorganization of ownership; reorganization of non-family leadership; preparing the business to be sold; putting the younger generation in charge of the business
- » The need for transparency and clear communication within, and between, each sector of the business
- » The fact that different questions pertain to each circle — that individuals' positions inside or outside the circles would determine the conversations they were a part of

We used the following figure in the meeting, first, to drive home the importance of understanding the makeup and goals of the three circles of any family business, and second, to give an overview of how complex the membership of these circles can be. This part of the discussion helped each person understand where they belonged in the family business, and who was in each circle.

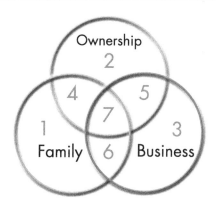

1. Family members with no ownership and who are not employed by the firm.
2. Owners and non-family members who do not work in the business.
3. Employees who just work in the business.
4. Family members and owners who do not work in the business.
5. Owners who work in the business.
6. Family members who work in the business but have no ownership.
7. Family members who have ownership in the business and work in the business.

After this all-inclusive meeting, we continued the introductory phase of succession planning by holding separate meetings with members of each sector of the family, ownership, and business circles.

THE FAMILY MEETING

We met first with family members, to explore their connection to the business, their values as a family, their contributions to the community, and how they saw their future involvement, or non-involvement, with respect to the business.

We talked about the concept of stewardship — of making things better for the generations to come. We discussed the optimal attitude of families when they own a business — the attitude that the resources of the business were not theirs to hold for their own good but theirs to protect, maximize, and hand down to the next generation of leaders. We emphasized that this was more of a *we* and less of a *me* conversation. We discussed the family's code of conduct and how the family could strengthen its bonds as a family.

This meeting gave individuals a voice. It helped them see themselves first and foremost as a family. It teased out their underlying values as a family for all to see and affirm.

And that was the ultimate aim of this initial family meeting: to give everyone involved an outlet to separate family from ownership and from business. We stressed that they should be a *family* when they were together as a family. We told them it was just as important — or more important — for a family to brag about how the kids were doing in school or sports as it was to think about the progress of the business owned by the family.

Melissa was initially confused about how we handled the family meeting. She was there as a family member, but her more immediate business concerns were ownership and the future of the company. We were pleased to see as the meeting went on, however, that she, too, was relieved to finally be focusing on what made their family great ... as a family.

We also met with Frank and his family, who obviously were concerned about what would happen to Frank's 7.5 percent ownership of the company. The same rule applied in this meeting. We talked about the family and its values and hopes and dreams, not about the business.

THE OWNERSHIP MEETING

Then we met with the two owners, Melissa and Frank. We explored several questions with them, including:

» How was the business doing in terms of its chief purpose — increasing shareholder value?

» What were the rules of engagement for the next generation?

» Were they as owners interested in reorganizing the business and the rules of ownership? If so, how would they clarify the rules of involvement in the business for both family members and business leaders? How would they make it clear that jobs and promotions depended not on a person's last name but on their skills, experience, and performance?

» Were they more interested in keeping the business going or in selling it?

» Was the business even ready to be sold? Were there any

interested parties? If no one was interested in buying it, would it be wise to automatically give it to the children to run? Why would they even think of handing it over to their children to run if the children didn't want to run it? Did they know for sure what the children wanted to do? And did they as owners really want to hand it over to the children if the latter weren't capable of running it? We stressed that the succession planning process should begin with a clear articulation of goals — both their personal and collective goals as owners

» What did they as owners wish to accomplish for the business, family members, key employees, and themselves as shareholders?

» How could we work with them so they not only identified and understood the common goals within the ownership group but also communicated them clearly to all three circles?

We said it was important to consider these questions because a business owner often has unspoken aspirations that certain key management personnel or family members will become the future leaders and owners of the business. We pointed out that if they hadn't consulted the persons involved to see if they shared their assumptions, conflict was likely to ensue in the event of an owner's illness or an accident or death.

Now that Melissa and Frank were beginning to articulate what they wanted to do, they could invite different perspectives from their trusted advisors (see page 74). Now that the transition process was out in the open, it was easier for them to see the kind of skills, experience, and support teams that would be needed by the next generation of leaders.

We also discussed the fact that it wasn't enough for ownership to articulate their goals. They also needed to explore these questions:

» Do these potential leaders have the skills necessary for success?

» Would it be worthwhile to conduct a management talent assessment?

» Should key employees be identified now?

» Can necessary skills be obtained through training or special assignments?

» What kind and level of support would they need to give to business leaders for them to succeed (mentoring, staff, knowledge)?

» How secure is my investment? Is my future tied to the success of this business?

» How do we enforce compliance on R.

Typical Goals

To the extent that a succession mirrors an arm's-length transaction, the business owner can begin to satisfy certain very important goals, which typically include:

» A reduction of the investment risk by obtaining some measure of liquidity

» The transfer of control to the next generation in proportion to the transfer of monetary risk

» A separation of ownership from management (being an owner does not equal telling management what to do)

(continues)

» Determining the fair market value of the company vs. the expectation of a discount by family members who may want to purchase the company

» Ensuring availability of funds for retirement and to provide financial equalization to other siblings

» Satisfaction that the business and its culture will survive and be maintained, if not improved

» The security of the company and ownership's investment if it is left in the company — should the investment be left in the company or taken out?

» Maximization of wealth for all shareholders

» Determining whether the company as it stands today is a sellable asset

The Question of Support

Sometimes asking owners about the support they need to give the next generation of leaders prompts them to seriously consider the idea of selling their business. If keeping the business running means they'll have to work eight-hour days as mentors to the next generation, they think, "What about Hawaii? What about my retirement plans? I want out."

But the same question may come as a relief to other owners. They may still feel motivated to work. They may be nervous about the unstructured nature of retirement. (That said, we watch carefully to see if they need help in understanding that "mentoring" doesn't mean "meddling.")

As the ownership meeting came to a close, we reiterated something that we had pointed out during the family meeting. We told Melissa and Frank that as owners they would be in most of the succession planning meetings that would follow, but family members not involved at a senior level in the business would not. Throughout the process, individuals would be invited to meetings based on where they fit in the overall scheme of things. A grandson who was a lower-level worker would not be invited into conversations at the senior level. We asked them, "What's a non-family MBA in the company going to think if a clerical worker is making decisions with him/her because of their family connection?"

THE BUSINESS LEADERSHIP MEETING

Finally, we met with the senior leadership of the business. We emphasized that family businesses are more likely to succeed when everyone involved understands that increasing profits — not creating jobs for members of the shareholders' family — is the main goal of the business. We emphasized the importance of setting up and communicating clear guidelines so members of the family were clear that holding down a job in the business would be the result of preparation, skill, and performance, not of being a member of the family, and that all positions would be reviewed on this basis, going forward, yearly.

We knew that treating employees well and making a difference in the community was very important to the owners. We wanted to get across to the owners, on the one hand, and the senior leaders in the business, on the other, that none of these desires would be accomplished if the business was not viable — if it did not make a profit.

This part of the discussion had an amazing effect. The fairness of this approach caused the senior leaders to relax and become more engaged in thinking about the company's succession planning process. What caused their sense of relief? Knowing they would have a fair crack at any promotions that came up — that a family member would not be parachuted in to take away what they had worked so hard to achieve.

FROM A LEGAL PERSPECTIVE

Many people start the succession planning process by talking to lawyers. However, it is important for the three circles of a family business — family, ownership, and business — to spend some time before talking to lawyers to clarify what their intent is vis-à-vis the family business. All three circles need to understand their intent, their goals, and the outcomes they wish to see. Being able to articulate these is the first step before having lawyers articulate such issues in a way that enables these things to happen. This is why the Family Business Counsel of Canada begins the discussion first at the level of intent before going on to the level of legal implementation.

Many lawyers are good at implementing a plan. They may be good at contributing ideas to save taxes or avoid corporate headaches. However, most lawyers are not trained to deal with family businesses and the management of the three circles of family, ownership, and business. Organizations like the Family Business Counsel of Canada can help because they recognize that although legal documents are important, harmonious succession is more important.

Rather than talk to lawyers first, make your plan first. Clients involved in any kind of planning should figure out what they want and then how to make it happen. By determining the way the family, owners, and business will look after succession, the first generation can ensure that their wishes are carried out.

If what you want is complex, the lawyers will let you know up front and you may have to change the plan to manage costs. Alternatively, you may find a way to carry out your wishes while organizing things differently from a corporate point of view.

CHAPTER 5

PHASE 2 / ASSESSMENT

In the previous chapter we showed how Phase 1 of the Succession Paradigm program established — for Melissa and Frank, the owners of Blooms, as well as for other family members and the company's senior leadership — the process of developing a succession plan, through the five phases of Introduction, Assessment, Alignment, Implementation, and Maintenance.

Now that everyone was on board with the planning process, it was time for us to find out exactly "what was the case" in terms of the three circles.

ASSESSING BLOOMS

VALUES AND FACT FINDINGS

The Family Business Counsel of Canada team drilled down for more details on the thinking and commitments of the people within the three circles associated with the company — the family, ownership, and business. We needed to understand the goals and track record of each circle, as well as any roadblocks to success or untapped opportunities for success. Part of this involved reviewing the legal and planning documents of the three circles. (See Appendix 1 of this book for details on these documents.)

The Importance of Confidentiality

Why is confidentiality so important? Because any leak that a company is considering its options could cause a dip in customer confidence in the company — and a feeling among those who might purchase the company that they can get it at a very low price. As well, gossip among family members, for example, could destabilize the work of employees, weakening the performance and value of the company.

Rumors can have harmful ripple effects, including decreased sales of products, loss of employees to competitor firms, less leverage in finding good employees, and a decrease in the value of the company in the eyes of potential purchasers. If confidentiality is broken, it is tough to get trust back. It's important to keep the conversations in each circle open and high level from meeting to meeting. What happens in the meetings should not be shared with outsiders.

DRILLING DOWN WITH THE FAMILY

We met with the family — composed of the owners, Melissa and Frank; Melissa's children and others from the family who were active in the business; and children and spouses and in-laws who were not active in the business. We invited to the meeting anyone in the family who understood the need for confidentiality. We made it clear that as others in the family grew into this understanding, they would become part of future family meetings.

This meeting repeated aspects of our Phase 1 introductory meeting, allowing us to assess the communication skills of the family and how seriously they were taking their role in the business and how open they were in talking to one another.

We emphasized the importance of inclusiveness in family discussions. We asked if any of them had ever played the popular party game of Telephone, in which a message is passed from one person to the next around the room. Of course the last person to receive the message, when asked what it is, says something that has absolutely no resemblance to the original message. We pointed out that the same thing would happen if we met with just a few family members and expected them to pass the information on to other family members.

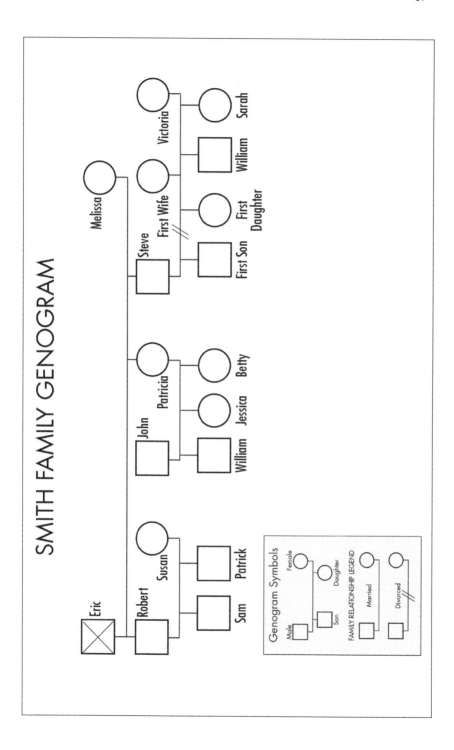

We went into greater depth about the three circles and had everyone self-assess where they thought they fit. We also asked them where they would like to be in five years. We talked about which conversations belonged in which circles. Our aim was to get a true understanding of the family dynamic. We knew the value of everyone in the family understanding that while family came first in family matters, business needed to come first in business matters. They began to see that observing the separation of church and state (family and business) was the only way to truly protect the interests of the family as a family and the interests of the business as a business.

In fact, assessing how well they were able to separate family from ownership and the business was the main goal of this meeting.

The next step was to help them create rules for family working in the business — and for clear communication about those rules. We found that in the case of Blooms Floral, as in many family businesses, the owners had an unwritten expectation that family members must work in the business if they wished to purchase shares. We discussed how this approach was not necessarily good for any of the three circles. We pointed out that we did agree with and understand the concept of keeping a vested interest in the business — but showed how this can be handled in ways that do not harm the circles.

Overall, we wanted to reinforce the importance of our introductory phase discussion that the family needed a place to be a family and talk about these issues, as well as more casually about family relationships, vacations, and how to deal with and support the next generation.

There were definitely some "aha moments," particularly among younger members of the family who were considering whether they wanted to become part of the business. They confirmed their understanding, as a result of this discussion, of this clear and overarching logic of family businesses: *The goal of business is to increase profits, because the goal of ownership is to increase shareholder value.*

They saw that the main goal of Blooms Floral was not to increase the wealth of family members by giving them a job because of their last name. The company was not some kind of exalted cash machine. Nor was it an employment agency.

ASSESSMENT QUESTIONS FOR THE FAMILY

Here are some of the questions we asked members of the family, in meetings, and, in many cases, individually:

» How can you work with other family members to separate business and ownership issues from family life?

» How does the company affect the family?

» What values does the family hold sacred?

» Where do you see this company in five years and ten years?

» Who should run the company? Why?

» Will the owner be bought out? If so, by whom?

» What is the company's stance on social issues? How does it give back to the community?

» What is stewardship?

» What do you owe future generations of this family?

» How are family members who don't work in the business seen by the business, the family, and ownership?

» Would you take a loan to buy shares in this company?

» If you had $20 million and ten years to live, what would you do?

» Who is family? Are spouses and in-laws included?

These questions were designed to focus family members on the succession planning process. They were designed to ignite a desire in each person to bring about the best results for everyone involved. We also brought participants together for brainstorming sessions as a further catalyst to buy-in. The Smith family was on board with the idea that clear and well-defined governance in each circle was the key to overall success.

What About You?

It's likely that you are an owner, which puts you in all three circles. As a member of the family circle, where do you see your company five and ten years from now? Are the values of your family manifested in the business? How do you see family members who don't work in the business?

It took several meetings for us to get the important things on the table and work through them. This process was not therapy, we said, but a process of learning and deciding how they wanted to move forward together.

We asked family members to exhibit the same openness when they talked matters over in their own family. Indeed, we stressed with Melissa and everyone in the meeting that her children would need to have separate meetings with their own family throughout the process. We said there could be decisions during the process in which each family had a vote. Voting decisions should be made privately, family by family, as a check against louder voices influencing the quieter ones.

DRILLING DOWN WITH OWNERSHIP

We also met separately with the owners, Melissa and Frank, to determine their goals and expectations for the business and for themselves, personally, over the next three to six years. We particularly wanted to know what they expected of those who might purchase shares in the company. What were the rules for other family members becoming part of ownership? Or was that even possible?

We role-played different situations with them. We asked them, for example, what would happen if they decided to sell the company but other members of the family wanted to purchase shares and work to keep the company "in the family" for future generations.

ASSESSMENT QUESTIONS FOR OWNERS

Here are some of the questions we asked the owners, in meetings, and, in some instances, individually:

- » How much time does the family as a management unit spend on various corporate issues?
- » Where do you think more time should be spent?
- » Is communication in the family business adequate? Where could it be improved?
- » Were the directors (if applicable) appointed or nominated to their position?
- » Should family members become part of the ownership of the company?
- » Should shares in the company be gifted to family members or sold to them?
- » Will you accept investment in the company from people outside the family?

Implimentation

» Does your shareholder agreement need review? Does it reflect the reality of how the business is doing and your needs?

» What is the return on investment of the leadership team of the business?

» Are you getting what you want from the business? *A. N.*

» How do you ensure that non-family executives remain engaged and motivated?

DRILLING DOWN WITH SENIOR BUSINESS MANAGEMENT

As for the senior management of the business, we met with the owners, the CFO, and all of the vice presidents to discuss the organizational structure of Blooms. Executives showed us their organizational chart (see page 73). We asked them how accurate the chart was against what actually happened in the company on a day-to-day basis. We wanted to know:

» How the company was being run

» Their understanding of ownership's goals

» How the company tracked progress

» The company's employee review process

» How their remuneration policies compared with industry standards

» The challenges the company faced and the opportunities it wished to pursue

» How company leaders felt about the way ownership handled family and business matters

» The business leadership's perceptions of the effect of the family on the business, whether negative or positive

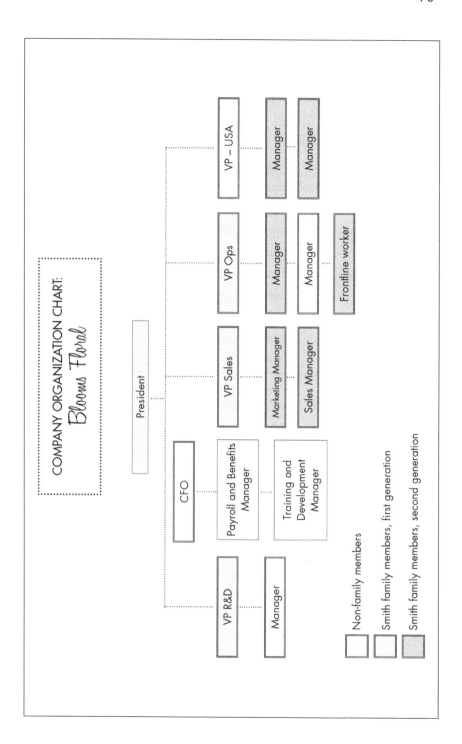

COMPANY ORGANIZATION CHART:
Blooms Floral

We asked the senior leaders for a list of goals for the business and then discussed them separately with the owners to see whether ownership and business were in sync on this crucial point.

MEETING WITH TRUSTED ADVISORS

The final step in this initial part of assessment was to meet with the owners' and the company's trusted advisors. As is the case in many family businesses, the owners, Melissa and Eric, had felt the need from time to time for an outside perspective on how they and their business were doing and for specific accounting and insurance advice. A senior partner from the company's accounting firm and an insurance advisor performed these roles for them. As well, given the entrepreneurial nature of Blooms Floral, they also leaned for advice on a long-time business friend and entrepreneur.

Most Trusted Advisors

We know we are unlikely to win an owner's full confidence and access to their plans and processes until we meet with their advisors.

Most Trusted Advisors (MTAs) are "gatekeepers." They may be professionals, such as a lawyer or accountant, whom the business owner has used for a while and who is trusted by the owner to provide objective input.

In our work with family businesses we work with their advisors to help them understand our Succession Paradigm approach to succession planning. We know that things proceed more smoothly when we engage external and trusted advisors in the conversation. The collaborative nature of this approach also builds the owners' trust in the planning process.

We indicated to the owners that we needed more details about Blooms Floral as part of the assessment phase. Sheldon Feinstein, the company's CFO, gave us access — at the direction of the owners and senior leadership, and under a non-disclosure agreement — to all of the legal documentation pertaining to employment contracts, buy-sell agreements, corporate policies, and governance, and, lastly, the family business owners' last will and testament. We also reviewed the insurance and investments of the owners and the business, as well as budget information, the balance sheet, and the auditors' report.

This was also the beginning of the data gathering process, using a proprietary **Fact Finder.** Where appropriate and applicable, we asked for copies of:

» Wills
» Family trusts
» Shareholder agreements, including buy-sell clause
» Employment contracts (family and key employees)
» Articles of Incorporation
» Corporate structure, including records of major events such as estate freezes
» Financial statements and five-year plan
» Contractual agreements with third party suppliers and providers
» Advance transfer pricing agreements with foreign divisions
» Personal guarantees

With this information in hand, we were able to begin determining options and opportunities for the owners and the business. We began to get a better grasp of:

» The type of company Blooms Floral is

» Whether the business was primarily entrepreneurial in nature (when ownership retired, would the business basically be over because driving force and expertise no longer existed in the business?)

» Or whether it was more complex and could exist independently of the leadership of the original owners

» The documents Blooms Floral had in place describing its structures and processes

» The names and contact information of all of its most trusted advisors from outside the business (the people it turned to for insurance, tax, legal, and financial advice)

» How secure the two owners were financially

» How revenue was generated by the business

» The assets of the business and which of them were to be passed on to family or to stay in the business

» Whether the business was sellable

In short, we looked at anything and everything that filled us in on where the company came from, where it was at present, and where it saw itself headed, both in the short term and the long term.

ASSESSMENT QUESTIONS FOR BUSINESS LEADERSHIP

Here are some of the questions we asked the owners and senior executives of the company, in meetings, and, in some cases, individually:

» What is the company's corporate governance and culture?

» How do you see this firm in the marketplace and how do you want it to be seen in the marketplace?

» Where is this firm headed and do you have a clear vision of how it will get there?

» What is your target market?

» How would you describe your industry?

» Do you know what your competitors are doing and how they are doing it?

» What do you think needs to be done in areas such as management, marketing, finance, and operations? Are the right people in place in these departments?

» What do you think is needed to make the board or family management more strategic, and why?

» Is the family business compliant with industry standards and laws?

» How does the business — and how do you, individually — compensate for changing conditions?

» When it comes to strategic execution, what do you think the five top priorities of the business should be?

» Is compensation commensurate with performance?

» What is the review process for capital expenditures?

TWO TYPES OF ASSESSMENT OF THE COMPANY'S CURRENT PLANNING

We continued to work with ownership, senior management of the business, and family members as individual groups to build clarity and vision going forward. We particularly wanted to understand the two basic types of planning of the business itself: its business planning and its succession planning.

PLANNING ASSESSMENT #1: BUSINESS PLANNING

The business leadership of Blooms, as with most family businesses, operated on the basis of business plans. These included budgets, capital expenses, a three-to-five-year business plan, and an organizational chart.

However, it's one thing to have plans and quite another to execute them. Was the company reaching its goals on a quarterly and yearly basis? What processes and benchmarks did the CEO and board (if in place) use in rating their progress? A good test for family businesses in assessing their planning is for them to estimate their likely market value if they were to sell.

We asked Blooms Floral:

> » Is your business sellable?
> » Would investors or purchasers be interested in the products, the customer base, and the leadership team?

Our questions sparked some interesting conversations.

We discovered that Eric's heart attack had cut short his and Melissa's discussion about a possible reorganization of the company. Their wills left everything to their three children equally in the event that both of them had passed on. The only person who had any knowledge of the Smiths' will was an elderly retired accountant who had played the role of trusted advisor but who would probably predecease Melissa.

It's not uncommon for owners to put plans into place for the next generation without asking them for their input. They shouldn't be surprised when there is little buy-in to their plans. We knew we needed to begin communicating the plan and the intent to Melissa's three children. We needed to work with the family and formulate a plan for what would be best for the business. We brought Frank into this discussion, too. He was surprised to learn that the three children were to inherit the business. He had been betting on Eric and Melissa to grow the business and maximize the worth of his shares. He wasn't so sure this would happen with the children at the helm.

Establishing organizational structure and strategies are only part of the assessment phase and the succession plan itself. Ensuring that the correct resources are in place is another big part of it. So is prioritizing essential programs and projects. The Family Business Counsel of Canada team researched the systems and schedule of priorities currently in place. We pointed out that programs and projects needed qualified staff to carry them out effectively and efficiently. Ensuring this, we said, would be part of the ongoing succession planning process.

The Notre Dame Approach

When we talk about business succession, we look at leadership development and capacity. We coach business leaders to ask, "Do we have the team and talent to take us forward in the years to come?" We stress that family businesses should think long term — not just today or even the next quarter but five to forty years down the road.

We sometimes illustrate this with how Notre Dame Cathedral in Paris was built by generation after generation of family workers. Those who worked on the footings of this colossal

> structure never saw much else of the building. They did what they did in the hope and faith that it would benefit generations to come.
>
> Most family businesses have no desire to form plans on the scale of building a cathedral, but they should think about what they're building for the future. This is not to say, however, that a business should automatically be continued by those generations. It might be about wealth generation.

We assessed the challenges faced by the family, the ownership, and the business. These included internal pressures within the family — specifically the current and future needs of the owners — and external pressures on the business given an increasingly competitive market.

Most of the people we talked to were committed to putting the most powerful and competitive organizational structure in place to drive the business plan and the succession plan.

We got down to the nitty-gritty with senior management, searching for all the right information in all the right places.

> » Accounting provided the Family Business Counsel of Canada team with financial projections five years out (some companies do not have this information)
> » We asked for management's profit tracker to determine if their targets were realistic and whether the company was achieving its objectives
> » We studied their cash flow projections to make sure there was enough revenue to maintain the infrastructure
> » We studied their expense reports

» We reviewed their business plans

» Another member of the team examined the company's balance sheets for the past three years

» One member of the team, a lawyer, examined employment contracts and compensation agreements. His research showed that the owners' shareholder agreement lacked a strong buy-sell agreement

» A financial expert on the Family Business Counsel of Canada team, along with the company's senior financial people and outside accountants, assessed the company's funding arrangements to determine whether they were current in terms of valuations

» We reviewed the compensation packages of key executives and all family members working in the business

» We brought in a business evaluator to determine the value and P/E (price to expense) ratios that should apply to a company within the floral industry based on contracts, reputation (goodwill), and profitability

» We stressed that we were working with senior team leaders and outside advisors in order to collaborate on what was best for the business. "We are not doing this *to* you but *with* you," we said. We added our own voice and ideas to those of the external experts when needed

» We wanted to know what the trends were historically for a business like Blooms Floral. We asked, "What is the proof that you'll be able to achieve the goals you're stating?"

It's also important how the management unit — whether made up of family members, non-family members, or both — works with other levels of management in developing processes. We talked to company leaders about the distinction between task and outcome. We recommended a shift to an emphasis on outcome. This would give the staff the flexibility they needed to be creative in building structures and processes and maintaining accountability.

We asked whether staff operated in seclusion or based on involvement. Involvement brings with it psychological ownership and commitment and creates value that is measurable. It was clear that the owners, as the founders and entrepreneurs behind the company, preferred to give people tasks based on their day-to-day sense of business needs and opportunities.

We showed the owners and business leaders the benefits of having senior leaders, managers, and staff focus on these two factors of outcome and involvement. We pointed out that personal growth within a company is always a value proposition and important to up-and-coming talent. Involving staff in decisions was one major way to gain their buy-in.

PLANNING ASSESSMENT #2: SUCCESSION PLANNING

The next step was to move from assessing the company's business planning to assessing its succession planning. What succession planning, if any, had been put together by ownership and leadership of Blooms Floral and how frequently was it reviewed?

The results of our assessment laid the groundwork for the owners and senior leaders to identify talent from within the business and outside the business. Melissa had made it clear to us that she was ready to step down from active leadership of the company. Frank had expressed his doubts about the younger generation's ability to maximize the worth of his shares. He was thinking of selling.

It became clear to the owners and senior management that the company would need a new president if it was to continue operating on a sound basis. We put it straight to the two owners. We asked them, "What would you do if the search process brought forth two candidates for the presidency, one from inside the business, whether a family member or not, and one from outside the business?"

By now Melissa and Frank understood the importance of separating business survival from family survival. They committed themselves to working with senior leadership to choose the leader who was best for the business.

We met not only with the owners but also with strategic management. We wanted to find out where they saw the organization five and ten years down the road. Our experience has shown that successful organizations listen to their staff. They are, after all, the key to the successful execution of any plans devised by the owners and senior leadership.

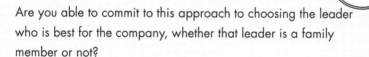

What About You?

Are you able to commit to this approach to choosing the leader who is best for the company, whether that leader is a family member or not?

We focused on long-term strategy with the family unit to understand how their current corporate governance was playing out and to determine their level of communication with each other. Our assessment made it clear to them that the family, ownership, and business leadership needed to rethink business priorities. The Family Business Counsel of Canada facilitator highlighted this need and set up tasks, committees, and accountability meetings to get it done.

It's amazing how much information we gathered during the assessment phase. A SWOT analysis of the firm was performed. This is an analysis that determines Strengths, Weaknesses, Opportunities, and Threats. We worked with senior management and the owners to define strategic objectives. We made it clear, in separate family, ownership, and business meetings, that each participant would be required to give thought to the process and be required to provide an assessment of what they envisioned themselves doing today, tomorrow, next week, next month, next quarter, and next year. It was crucial for individuals to develop their own strategies and objectives.

We gauged the motivation and commitment level of senior leaders. We knew this information would directly impact our views — and more importantly the owners' views — of these leaders. Were they in the running to continue leading the company? Were they candidates for promotion as part of the succession process? Or did they no longer fit in the company's future? Often during this phase of succession planning some in leadership will opt out of the company because they feel uncomfortable, personally or professionally, with the new direction. There's nothing wrong with this; in fact, it shows that the succession planning process is doing its work.

We asked where Blooms Floral wanted to be in five years and in ten years. We stressed the need for all three circles to have clear and measurable benchmarks by which the individuals involved could assess their own progress.

At Blooms Floral, as in so many businesses, succession planning was not explicit and recorded on paper. Rather, it existed, in general terms, in the minds of the owners. They had not articulated their view of the future leadership of the company to other business leaders. Ownership's approach was to dictate tasks, not invite people to buy into a plan to achieve objectives.

This is a far cry from companies that do have detailed and written plans, constituting, in effect, a corporate will: a carefully crafted statement containing very specific steps to be taken in the event of a major change. Such companies may even recruit the help of finance to help them understand the effects of their dreams or decisions on the budget process. These leaders are able to see their vision and plan in action.

Assessing the succession planning of Blooms Floral involved looking at each position of the company and how it was supposed to contribute to its goals, and then examining the people actually in those positions to see if they were a match. Business in general is often lax on this issue of making sure the right people are in the right positions. Family businesses tend to score even lower on "fit" because they often struggle to make the tough decisions on positions held by family members primarily because they are family.

Corporate Wills

Although "corporate will" is not a technical term, it is possible to have a will for a corporation.

Most companies execute a shareholder agreement, which dictates many of the terms of how shareholders must govern themselves with respect to the corporation. The corporate will aspect of this agreement covers off what will happen in the case of the death of a shareholder. It will dictate:

» The price of that shareholder's shares or how the price of the shares will be calculated
» The method for transferring shares (sale, redemption, or a combination)

> » The form of payment
> » The timing of the payment
> » And any terms specific for future payment
>
> The corporate will is a crucial part of the shareholder agreement because it ensures that unwanted beneficiaries of a deceased's estate do not end up with any form of control of the corporation.
> Life insurance is commonly used to fund these provisions so the necessary proceeds for buying out the estate of the late shareholder exist at exactly the time they are needed.

We set up processes for Blooms Floral to assess talent honestly and hold all positions accountable to achieve results. We recommended that they take the following five steps.

THE FIVE STEPS IN ASSESSING TALENT

STEP 1 / IDENTIFY KEY AREAS AND KEY POSITIONS
Identify which positions, if left vacant, would be detrimental to the family business.

STEP 2 / IDENTIFY THE CAPABILITIES NEEDED FOR KEY AREAS AND KEY POSITIONS
Make sure the profiles of appropriate positions are in place. The focus here is on positions, not on the people currently holding those positions.

The questions to ask are, "What does a person do in this position? What if this position didn't exist? Do we need it in this company? What are the responsibilities and expected outcomes of the person in this position? What experience, talents, and skill sets are needed in the role?" Only after exploring these questions are the names of people to be brought back into it.

STEP 3 / *IDENTIFY INTERESTED EMPLOYEES AND ASSESS THEM AGAINST THE CAPABILITIES NEEDED*

Develop an inventory of employee skills and experience to ensure that a pool of trained staff is available for key areas and positions. This goes back to having a defined corporate plan in place in order to build organizational capacity and put the right people in the right seats or leadership roles.

STEP 4 / *DEVELOP AND IMPLEMENT SUCCESSION AND KNOWLEDGE TRANSFER PLANS*

Institute succession planning and knowledge transfer programs and processes. Incorporate responsibility for conducting succession planning and knowledge transfer activities in performance management agreements. This is about building corporate capacity.

STEP 5 / *EVALUATE EFFECTIVENESS*

Are the values and quantifiable targets being met? Are we meeting our plan? Is the plan a stretch? What's the proof?

• • •

Now we were ready to work with Blooms Floral on the next phase of its succession planning: aligning the family, business, and ownership circles.

FROM A LEGAL PERSPECTIVE

At the end of the previous chapter we emphasized
how important it is to focus on intent, goals, and outcomes
before lawyers are assigned to draw up documentation.
That said, it is important to bring lawyers into the discussion early in the succession planning process.

Most families go to their lawyer after problems begin. As
a result, fixing problems becomes more costly, both financially and emotionally.

Imagine the strain of a lawsuit on a family. A recent article
describes a case in which one of two brothers passed away
four years earlier at the age of 75. Although this man's estate
is sizeable, it is primarily made up of a couple of pieces of
real estate. His brother and children have been fighting over
his estate ever since he died. According to the article, their
legal bills in this "relatively simple case," which has had
"only" fourteen motions to date, is $4.4 million.

Could this have been avoided with good planning?
Definitely. Much of the strife could have been avoided if the
lawyers had been involved with the family earlier, with the
intent of educating the family.

CHAPTER 6

PHASE 3 / ALIGNMENT

As our work with Blooms Floral continued, the succession planning picture was coming into focus. By completing the assessment phase, we had a good understanding of the vision of the three circles — family, ownership, and business — vis-à-vis the family business. We also had a preliminary understanding of the "talent pool" in the business — of the strengths and weaknesses of individuals in middle and senior management.

The next phase — alignment — involved bringing together and harmonizing the understandings, processes, and plans of all three circles associated with Blooms Floral. Alignment is about getting all of the parts working together using the same process for the same purpose. This cannot happen until the key players have a clear vision regarding the future — both their own and that of the three circles.

We were pleased that key people within the three circles were now thoroughly engaged in thinking about the succession planning process. We heard from many that they appreciated the openness of the process and were relieved they could discuss issues within and between the three circles.

In fact, if the assessment phase prompted *engagement*, the alignment phase prompted *creative energy*. Instead of running for emotional cover when gaps within and between the circles revealed themselves, people were passionate about finding ways to close those gaps. The family, owners, and business were building a solid foundation for ongoing communication.

WORKING WITH THE TEAMS

To begin the alignment phase, we worked with the members of the three circles to set up a smaller team for each circle. We assured those who were not chosen to be on the teams that they would receive regular progress reports and have ample opportunity to add their input. We let the business team know we were relying on them to "take care of business" on a day-to-day basis. We continued to support them, but let them know our focus for the time being would be on the family and ownership circles.

This focus was important because once the rules of ownership are clear, some of the members may decide to make a change, creating some gaps in the company. We said we would return to discuss alignment with them once we had aligned the family and ownership circles.

In the case of Blooms Floral, the owners were part of both the family and the ownership meetings. At first they questioned this process as wasteful duplication, but they understood our rationale for separate meetings when we said the meetings would concentrate on different goals and *then* the teams would be brought together.

In the meeting with the ownership team — consisting of Melissa, Frank, and two trusted advisors: a lawyer in Melissa's case and an accountant in Frank's — we confirmed the owners' desire to step down from business leadership and to sell their shares.

In the meeting with the family team — consisting of the two owners, Melissa's three children, and their spouses and children who were of an age to understand the concept of confidentiality — we confirmed the family's view of its history and values, including its ongoing contributions to the community. Our aim, with respect to the family circle, was to be as inclusive as possible.

Next we brought the family and ownership teams together to discuss gaps in assumptions, hopes, and goals of the people involved.

Melissa and Frank clarified the conclusions of the ownership team:

» Both owners wanted to transition out of their current roles — Frank as an advisor and Melissa as president — as soon as it was feasible for the company

» Both Frank and Melissa would remain on the board

» Melissa wanted to sell her shares over the next five years, preferably to her three children, who were working in the company

» Frank, for tax and security reasons, preferred to keep his shares in the company; however, he felt that Melissa's children currently lacked the business acumen to keep Blooms profitable. He persisted in his strategy that he would probably sell his shares if the children were put in more senior positions

» Owning shares in the company would not automatically mean any new shareholders would be given positions or promotions in the company. From now on, merit,

ongoing training, and experience would be factored into
employment and leadership decisions
» Any shares left open after the children made their
purchases would be offered to other family members
first, management second, and outside investors third

Members of the family team brought several things out into the
open, including:

» Two of Melissa's children, Robert and Patricia,
were interested in continuing with the company in
their positions as VP of Sales and VP of Research &
Development, respectively. But both were also interested
in becoming president. And both said they wanted to
purchase shares from the owners once they understood
the process, price, and commitment needed. As part of
the succession planning process, they were beginning to
understand that while ownership has its privileges, it also
has its risks
» The third child, Steve, wanted to stay in the company in
his current position as manager of marketing. He had
no ambition to rise higher in the business but did want
to own a percentage of the shares as security for his
children

Like the flowers it was expert in cultivating, the Smith family
flourished when the lines of communication were open. Both of
the owners and Melissa's children were relieved to be talking about
issues they had always kept to themselves.

The alignment challenge in this case was: How could structures and processes be put in place that honored the children's desires and goals while making sure Frank was comfortable with how his investment would be handled?

The next step was to present a game plan to the family and ownership teams and then confirm that plan in a joint meeting between the two teams.

This became possible two months later, after several individual and group meetings with the Family Business Counsel of Canada team that focused on closing the gaps between the two circles.

THE GAME PLAN

Frank and Melissa agreed that Sheldon Feinstein, the company's CFO, would replace Melissa as president in three months' time. He would be given a guaranteed two-year term, during which he would mentor Robert and Patricia to see whether either or both had what it took to be president. For their part, Robert and Patricia would be required to take MBA courses part-time to strengthen their overall knowledge of business and to deepen their understanding of finance.

Melissa decided she would put 25 percent of her shares up for sale to her children within a year, and the rest within five years. This way she could keep control while determining whether her children wanted to take the risk of having a vested investment in the company and take on the responsibilities that went with ownership. Frank decided to leave his 7.5 percent in the company for two years, after which he would keep his investment in the company if he felt confident in the direction and the leadership of the company going forward.

ENTER, THE BUSINESS CIRCLE

As mentioned, we had put discussions with the business team on hold. After all, how could the business fulfill its role — to implement the succession vision of the family and ownership — if the family and ownership circles were not yet aligned?

We now relayed to business circle team — consisting of the interim president and all of the vice presidents, including Robert and Patricia — where the family and owners stood in terms of the business and its future. There were looks of relief around the room as executives heard two messages loud and clear: first, that the business was going to be operated on business terms with no meddling by the owners or family members, and second, that skills, experience, and commitment, not genetics, would determine who was promoted to more senior positions. Robert and Patricia were relieved, too, because they wanted it out in the open that they held their positions because they were good at what they did.

The president and vice president of human resources put a process in place to cross-train Robert and Patricia. For their part, they welcomed the opportunity to develop their vision of the future of Blooms Floral and present it to the ownership group and the board of advisors.

We pointed out that the owners and family had agreed that workers and managers — whether they were family members or not — would be moved upward in the business only if their experience and skills had grown to fit the needs and responsibilities of those more senior positions. Otherwise, we said, the business would end up with weak, inadequate, and unsustainable management at the top. And we stressed that the family businesses that did the best over time were open to hiring outside talent when the talent, skills, and experience were not present, or could not be developed in time, in house.

We also discussed the need to balance the process of *building* leaders and *buying* them. To succeed long term, we said, the leaders of Blooms Floral would need to blow on the sparks of leadership talent within the company while also searching for new leaders from outside the firm. Blooms wisely chose a blended approach to succession planning. The aim was to keep the business in family hands, as warranted, while making sure strong leaders and support people were in place to guide those family hands.

Fundamental Change

At some point, every business comes to the realization that fundamental change is needed. Whatever the reason for bringing about change, the CEO or family leader usually realizes that it will be demanding and stressful and will require a prolonged effort to bring it about on a sustainable basis.

On the issue of finding new executives to replace owners who are running the business, we stress the reality of the natural business cycle of most companies. They are often started and run by entrepreneurial visionaries. The next leaders often need to be strong on structure and processes. However, down the road, these leaders may need to be replaced by visionaries; otherwise, the company may become stagnant and miss new opportunities in a new business environment.

Most leaders look to replace themselves with leaders who are like them. Once they understand the different sets of skills necessary for new leaders, they can understand that it's not personal — it's the evolution of the business cycle. Ego can get in the way here.

A big question early in the succession planning process is whether a team is in place to support the new style of leadership that is being sought. Typically, the founding owner of a business holds meetings in which the leadership team is told what to do. How is such a team going to react when the next president and CEO asks them for their opinions on what the company should do? They'll probably think it's a trick question!

We understand what goes wrong in many business succession transformations. If a family business does not address the following fundamental issues, it is almost guaranteed to fail as a business in the long term. The issues are:

» Lack of quality communication
» Lack of strategic planning
» Failure to select the right talent and apply it strategically (because the business owner wants to avoid conflict within the family, not realizing that this is a major cause of conflict and rivalry)
» How the new regime will sustain and grow the family business, and how they will they organize and reorganize during the transition process
» What conflicts will arise and how will they be dealt with
» The support mechanisms that are or are not in place
» Accountability

With the three circles now harmonized and working smoothly together, we were ready to work with Blooms Floral on the next phase of succession planning: implementation.

FROM A LEGAL PERSPECTIVE

In the alignment phase, you must be certain of who your quarterback is. Someone must look at all of the documents and make sure all are aligned with the three circles of family, ownership, and business. The documents will be distributed to all interested parties for review and comments. Not only must the documents be aligned with each other, they also must be aligned with the vision of the family, the owners, and the business as everyone in these circles moves forward.

It is important at this point to be inclusive. Everyone should have a chance to examine the documents. This will help everyone feel involved in the process — because they really *are* involved. The process gives lawyers an opportunity to revise the legal documents if anything is out of alignment with what they thought would happen or would like to see happen. It is always best for people to put these concerns out there early in order to avoid fighting, discontent, and, worst case scenario, law suits later on. It is more effective to give your legal team the clear outcomes you are hoping for because they can then provide you with the best options to get you there.

CHAPTER 7

PHASE 4 / IMPLEMENTATION

It is often difficult to tell where the alignment phase (covered in the previous chapter) ends and the implementation phase begins. In a sense, the implementation of the family and owner's vision begins when the business circle is aligned to the family and ownership circles. Just as the *what* and *why* flow from the family and ownership circles, so the *how* becomes the purview of the business circle.

Businesses operate on the basis of stating goals and then determining how to reach them in how they put together the people, goals, measurement tools, and accountability structures of the business. Once the business team knows the intents and goals of ownership and ownership's policy on family involvement in the business, it can determine how to set up the business and succession plans to meet these intents and goals. Yes, it's true that a business must have its own vision, but that vision is subsidiary to the vision of ownership and family.

The implementation phase is a multidisciplinary process that also acts as a guide in the transition process. Thus it affords the owners and senior leadership clarity of vision and comprehension, enabling them to manage effectively going forward.

This phase occurs in stages and requires the assistance of a lawyer and insurance person as well as the firm's most senior accountant. A lawyer with expertise and experience in taxation law will guide the rest of the team and the family. This plan must be realistic and will have involved the entire family throughout the process. It must also involve professional advisors, shareholders, partners, strategic employees, and all major shareholders in the business. Remember, the goal is the total buy-in of all concerned.

Revisiting the game plan created by the family and owners with the Family Business Counsel of Canada team, the CFO of Blooms Floral moved into the president's role and worked with the owners to set up a board of advisors — something that had been sorely lacking at Blooms Floral since its initial expansion from a one-store business. The board was put together by having Melissa choose an advisor, Frank choose an advisor, and then the two owners choose a third advisor together. This created a five-member board, ensuring that there would not be tie votes. Robert and Patricia were invited to attend meetings as part of their development. The board's task was to ensure that:

» The owners' investment remained secure
» The wishes and intent of the family and owners for the business were protected
» The business put processes, as well as measurement and accountability mechanisms, in place to make sure all of this happened
» The executive team was held accountable to the business plan

Some Points About Implementation

» The implementation phase can take months or even years, depending on business owners' timetable and the complexity of the business. There will be many re-runs and amendments as a result of seeking total buy-in from all parties. We advise families and companies to strive for total buy-in through a combination of good communication, clarity, and transparency. This approach helps reduce or eliminate conflict and rivalry

» Alternatives and choices may disappear if no action is taken. This is both inefficient and counter-productive. Leaving business succession to chance could allow someone else to decide what happens to the business, potentially at significant cost to everyone concerned. As opportunities decrease, given the mismanagement of the succession plan, ownership and family may be left with one choice: to sell the business

» It is important to have the right conversations with the right groups on the right time line:

   o Shareholders should participate in five- to ten-year plans
   o Executives must think one to five years down the road
   o The management team typically looks at daily operations one to twelve months ahead

THE SUCCESSION PLAN

A year into our work with Blooms Floral (note that some companies may take six months to get to this point, others eighteen months) we had gathered a great deal of information and referenced it both internally against our own resources and externally against a wide array of material publicly available. We had collaborated with members of the three circles to align the vision and goals of the three circles of family, ownership, and business. We were now in a position to write a draft Succession Paradigm succession plan.

To do this, we assessed the talent pool again, but in a more targeted way this time now that we could do so based on the company's business strategy. The Family Business Counsel of Canada and the president or general manager and their designee met with each senior and middle manager, whether they were family members or not, to better understand their skills and experience, their clarity regarding their role in the business, and their vision of themselves and their department going forward.

We pulled together the skills, projections, and ideas gathered in the assessment and alignment phases, paying special attention to:

» Corporate governance — the makeup and function of the board of advisors and the reporting function of the president and senior executives

» The future relative to the past, outlined in a detailed business plan

» The roles and responsibilities of current executives, managers, and employees

» Alternative persons for those and possibly new roles

» Contingency plans for leading the company in the case of resignations or the incapacity or death of the owners and executives

» Quantifiable systems for evaluating progress, including cash flow projections, financial projections, and profit tracker reports

We sent the plan to the three teams (family, ownership, and business) detailed for their area or circle with an overview of the others. The board of advisors received a complete, detailed plan. Then we brought all of these parties together to make modifications where appropriate, based on information that had surfaced in the earlier alignment meetings and from their feedback after reviewing the plan. Then we prepared to revise the plan and move the process forward.

The plan highlighted the type of person the owners believed would be most capable to lead the firm. It included profiles of current leaders in the firm, including Robert and Patricia, indicating their training, experience, and performance, as well as their goals for themselves as leaders. The challenge, we said, was to look at management relative to the new performance model, so business leaders could put the right people in the right positions, right up to the top spot.

The plan also included a workable and sustainable organizational chart as developed by the business circle team at the end of the alignment phase. The idea was that available talent would be harnessed, but qualified and experienced people outside the company would be assessed, too.

It was agreed that the board would meet three or four times a year to review the progress of the business and succession planning and make recommendations regarding the future performance of the business.

The board was given the responsibility of being a knowledge asset to the president and executive team. The length, breadth, and quality of the advisors' experience provided leaders with a clear picture of the best practices, industry-wide, of businesses similar to Blooms Floral. The board was also given the responsibility of reviewing the president's performance as well as the company's vision, budgets, senior human resources issues, financing, and opportunities to sell to another firm or to acquire other businesses.

Advice and Execution

It is important for a business to understand and observe a critical distinction between the role of a board of advisors and the role of management. The distinction can be summed up in a few words: Boards advise and management manages. We often review with owners and leaders how inefficient and unproductive it is when advisors play politics and try to manage a company from the board room.

Next, the president, his senior executives, and representatives from the board of advisors set up a process for Robert and Patricia to prove they could take on greater responsibility. The two were now enrolled in their MBA courses and met regularly with the president for mentoring and coaching. The president gave quarterly reports on their progress in meetings of the owners and the board of advisors.

We emphasized in meetings within and between the three teams (family, ownership, and business) that human potential is unlimited given the right circumstances and stimuli. The more people achieve, the more enthusiastic and motivated they are. And we filled the teams in on what to expect, and how to deal with, the inevitable shift in staffing in the aftermath of the alignment process.

A SHIFT IN STAFFING

The alignment phase enabled the president and his executives to:

» Ask people in senior positions if they could commit to the new structures, processes, and the role they were being asked to perform

» Detect a lack of fit in some people — workers whose skills and commitments were not supportive of the changes. Management discussed the fit question with these workers and let them know how they would need to change to support the direction of the company. In most cases, these workers were moved to a new responsibility within the company and monitored for their suitability in that new role. In other cases, they were let go to find a better fit for their talents and desires

» Check on the level of value, respect, and caring that everyone was feeling for the company. Leaders noted that for some individuals in the company, including some in senior management, the changes "didn't feel like home anymore." A few mid-level managers opted out of the company and looked for work elsewhere

THE MINDS OF A LEADER

We spent several meetings with the owners and the business team discussing the type of leader Blooms Floral needed to ensure ongoing growth. We used the insights of *Five Minds for the Future*, a book by Harvard University's Howard Gardner, to explore the ideal attributes of a new leader. As an expert on different types of intelligence, Gardner categorizes these five minds as:

» The disciplined mind
» The synthesizing mind
» The creative mind

» The respectful mind
» The ethical mind

Specifically, with the owners' support, we encouraged the president and his senior executives to look inside and outside the company for presidential candidates. We said that, based on Gardner's model, these candidates should be people who were *disciplined* — people who continually honed their skills to the point that they were valued in their industry for their insights, judgments, and opinions.

We emphasized that the business needed someone who was able to take diverse gifts and interests and *synthesize* them into a powerful, unified approach to securing the company's future. It also needed a leader who was not paralyzed by what was or what is but who was *creative*, dreaming new dreams for the company.

With the owners' stated goals in mind, we said they should be on the lookout for leaders who *respected* people of different backgrounds, interests, and skills, and who consciously followed *ethical* guidelines in their profession and the community — people who saw business as a means to the greater good of society.

Going a few steps further than Gardner, we added that they should watch for leaders who were *analytical*, aware of what they should pay attention to and what they could ignore, and who were *driven* to achieve goals. Finally, the right leader for Blooms would be able to play the role of mentor to those who reported to him or her — someone who acted as a steward of the company's history and resources for the sake of the next generation.

We asked the senior team working with us who in the company's senior management had the ability to teach, which is a tremendous asset and value to the business both now and in the years to come.

Doing this exercise helped them see Patricia in a new light. Although Robert was stronger at external relations — making connections with major players in the industry and sizing up companies that were for sale — Patricia had a solid record of training and developing workers, most of whom were still with the company.

We urged the president and his senior executives to be alert to recognizing role players in the company who were good at what they did and wished to continue in those roles. The fact that someone did not want to move to a more senior position did not necessarily mean they were not motivated, we said. Moving them up could be wrong for them and for the business.

"The Future"

To help the owners and business leaders get a bead on the type of leader they were looking for, we helped them identify and develop a solid understanding of the most significant challenges the company and its industry were likely to face over the next four to six years, and the skills and experiences the CEO would need to lead the company in that context.

The word "future" is often used rather casually in business. In a corporate transition, the future could be "the foreseeable future," but it could also be defined as the next three to five years. The Succession Paradigm approach focuses on identifying the future as measurable, quantifiable, and definable. In our approach, the process of matching talent to the various roles and responsibilities of a company is benchmarked against these standards.

We relayed one last point from Gardner's discussion — that a leader, while building on what has been done in the past, knows that the future requires a different mindset and different skills. This makes ongoing education in technology a prerequisite. Family businesses need the support of new disciplines, technologies, and marketing strategies.

A STRONG FOUNDATION

Almost two years into our work with Blooms Floral, things were definitely looking up. Momentum was being carried by the leadership of each circle.

> » A strong foundation had been built and a new direction had been set
> » Everyone involved knew the time lines of the owners in terms of their retirement plans. They were aware of Robert and Patricia's leadership ambitions and the desire of all three children to purchase shares from the owners
> » Leadership of the company was in the capable hands of Sheldon Feinstein. He, the owners, and members of the advisory board were actively assessing Robert and Patricia's efforts to land the top spot and were also scouting top talent outside the company

In fact, the president got approval to hire a leader from outside the company to become vice president of US Operations. This was a strategic move, because the person chosen would be qualified to take over the top spot if neither Robert nor Patricia was deemed to be ready.

As part of the implementation of the succession plan, we helped the president and his senior executives define the skills needed for the middle management team levels. These levels are important because as talent moves upward, a void is created below. We worked with the VP of HR to define an optimal organizational structure with as little fat as possible (following the approach of retain the top ten and eliminate the bottom ten).

Who was accountable to whom and for what was the new company mantra. Our model outlined what was needed to make a smooth and seamless transition from one layer of leadership to the next. We explained that because business is highly competitive, a company could not afford the luxury of holding on to more employees than it needed. It is just not economically viable or efficient.

In assessing the talent pool against the new strategy, the business circle determined which managers and workers had leadership experience or potential, and, crucially, desire. Who was buying in to the succession planning process? Change was in the air. Who adapted to that fact with courage? Who reacted by holding on to past procedures for dear life?

This was all part of the process of creating a match between the company's future needs and the aspirations, skills, and abilities of its current employees. It prompted the president to begin looking, with Steve, who was recognized as an excellent marketing manager, for people outside the company to fill gaps that had been identified on the marketing team.

Through this process the company was able to identify who was ready in the event of contingencies and what type of development was needed to get people ready to step up in the event of a contingency. We pointed out that simply moving people up one level was easy. The harder, and lengthier, task was to identify talent and capability for *future* upward movement.

A Leadership Exercise

We sometimes take the owners of a family business through a critical leadership exercise. We ask them to role-play a situation in which the firm hits a period of economic crisis. We ask them to imagine the way current leadership would handle it.

Then we have them role-play dealing with the challenge the way an outside candidate with a different set of experiences and skills might handle it.

This is definitely "play," because neither the owners nor we know exactly what would happen in a situation like this in real life. Owners find this exercise very useful, because it casts light on the strengths and weaknesses of current leadership.

TECHNICAL MATTERS

CONTRACTS, PROCESSES, AND PROCEDURES

We sought the advice of Blooms Floral's lawyer to help us and the board of advisors deal with contracts, processes, and procedures. The lawyer drew up employment contracts for each executive to sign; completed the reorganization documentation; and drafted a new buy-sell agreement to govern the owners' sale of shares.

The Family Business Counsel of Canada representatives reviewed and implemented, with the help of the outside lawyer, the accountant, and the new CFO of Blooms, the legal structures, financial models, and risk management vehicles that we had designed and created specifically for the owners.

SHAREHOLDER AGREEMENT

Succession planning at Blooms did not take place in isolation from the larger issue of the business owners' overall financial security. This is why an updated shareholder agreement was so important.

A shareholder agreement determines the rules of ownership, the rights of succession, how the shareholders should interact with the management of the business, and what happens in the case of catastrophic events. It should address who can hold shares; how and under what conditions shares can be sold or transferred; and who they can be sold or transferred to.

In the case of Blooms, we included in the revised shareholder agreement a funding mechanism in the event of the disability or death of the owners by issuing both of them with a life insurance policy paid for and owned by the business. The family business was the beneficiary as well.

Why is having a strong shareholder agreement so important? Consider what would happen, for example, if a company faced a dire liquidity need or one of the above situations revealed weak direction concerning competent successor management. A distress sale might be the only answer, meaning the firm would be sold at a lower price. This point highlights how crucial a good succession plan is in retaining talented workers and increasing the value of the business for shareholders.

As a side note, some investors may not be content with being passive investors and may want some form of voting privilege. This adds fuel to the proverbial fire. A strong, clearly defined shareholder agreement is definitely needed.

For more details on the makeup of a shareholder agreement, see "From a Legal Perspective" at the end of this chapter, as well as Appendix 2.

TAXES

Planning early also helps reduce the tax impact of ownership changes and ensures a smooth and successful transition of the business to the next generation or new owners. Business valuators agree that a successful plan will also help enhance the overall value of the business today. Continuity and consistency are cornerstones of good planning.

The benefits to companies and owners who plan properly include:

» Survival and growth of the business
» Preservation of personal and family wealth
» Preservation of family harmony
» Minimization of estate and income taxes
» Facilitation of retirement
» Confidence in the marketplace with creditors and bankers
» Owners enabled to support philanthropic interests

This section of the plan is exceedingly important, especially if the business owner is planning to retire or is taking a precautionary approach to the future of the business in the event of their illness or death. Proper succession planning will significantly impact the financial future of the business owner, the business itself, and all those with a financial stake in the business (family members, partners, shareholders, and employees).

During the implementation phase, outside advisors are necessary to ensure that all issues are properly addressed, and the Succession Paradigm lines all the procedures and processes up in a logical way. Advisors to be consulted include lawyers, accountants, financial/ estate planners, and life insurance representatives. Each advisor will have his or her own area of expertise and will be able to provide necessary pieces of the puzzle.

RESIGNATIONS, FIRING, DEATH

The death of a shareholder/manager, resignation of the top leader, or hiring of a new leader can threaten the success of a business. Such events raise the questions, Who will manage the business? Who will buy the shares? Where will the money come from to buy the business? Will the shares be gifted to family members? What will the tax consequences be? Where will the money come from to pay those taxes?

Transition of leadership may take a year or more to complete. The company is at its most vulnerable when not in capable hands — for example, when one CEO moves out and another moves in. When leadership hangs in the balance, banks get nervous, customers switch allegiances, staff spends too much time worrying and not working ... and on it goes.

Owners or CEOs who are slated by the succession plan to move out of day-to-day management sometimes don't go quietly. This can destabilize executives who are loyal to them. It is important to help the CEO and founders with their exit strategy, or to find a place for them in the business once the transition has occurred.

What About You?

Do you have a shareholder agreement? Has everyone signed it? Does it need to be revised? All too many times, shareholder agreements have been drafted but not finalized. Yet they are at the very heart of the financial stability of the business.

This process can be daunting. Today, to help families make

successful transfers, some financial advisors are quietly broadening their approach. They are part of a new movement that is urging families to focus on passing on values as well as valuables to successive generations. "That's where parents typically fall down," says Paul Binnion, Clark Capital Management Group. "They just pass the money without passing the values involved in its creation."[*]

THE BENEFITS OF SUCCESSION PLANNING

Remember the story at the beginning of this book in which one of the authors, Michael Lobraico, ran afoul of his own family's poor succession planning? Suffice it to say that lack of communication in how shares are to be split in a family business, especially between children who have varying degrees of involvement in the business, can cause sibling rivalry and conflict. A strong succession plan would have made all the difference in Michael's case.

Insurance can be set up to create an "instant estate" that can be used to provide for children who are not active in the business, thus creating equity in the family. All too often we find that the family leader or CEO does not apply fairness in the division of assets. In many cases, the CEO or family leader puts more importance on the business than on the family. This is how they protect and feed their families.

Many forward-thinking executives have effectively used equity carve-outs as an organizational tool that allows them to raise capital by selling equity at higher rates sometime in the future by spinning off divisions of the firm.

The creation of holding companies and operating companies

---

[*] Quoted in *The Christian Science Monitor*, March 13, 2006.

allows for effective transfer of funds up through an organization, benefiting different types of shareholders at different levels.

The shares of an operating company could be owned by one or more holding companies where each holding company has its own shareholders. This is an effective way to distribute capital gains. If there is more than one operating company, each operating company's shares can be owned by a holding company. We also see operating companies that are separate from their real estate holdings.

We discuss this structure in detail as a possible option with the CEO and in conjunction with his or her legal and professional team.

Examining corporate structure helps identify levels of responsibility, but more importantly it helps devise a financial model. In this way we can create levels through which cash flows at advantageous levels of taxation.

We find that some members would prefer to cash out and others would prefer a combination of cash and shares and lucrative renewable employment contracts. Everyone has different aspirations, depending on where they fit into the organizational chart and the stage of life they have reached.

The Family Business Counsel of Canada team assesses the corporate governance of a company. This entails reviewing a list of officers and directors together with a list of their duties, including a list of senior management and their corresponding duties. Effective governance structures can help maintain a healthy family and business by promoting open communication and reducing rivalry and conflict.

We helped Blooms Floral to: evaluate the effectiveness of its governance structures; design new ones or implement modifications to existing ones; create policies; articulate the family and owners' values and vision; and clearly state the business's mission and strategy.

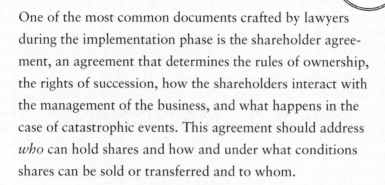

FROM A LEGAL PERSPECTIVE

One of the most common documents crafted by lawyers during the implementation phase is the shareholder agreement, an agreement that determines the rules of ownership, the rights of succession, how the shareholders interact with the management of the business, and what happens in the case of catastrophic events. This agreement should address *who* can hold shares and how and under what conditions shares can be sold or transferred and to whom.

This agreement's buy-sell provisions outline certain circumstances under which one shareholder is obliged to buy shares and another is obliged to sell them to that buying shareholder. These events are:

» Death
» Disability
» Marital breakdown
» Bankruptcy
» Mental incapacity
» Disputes among the shareholders

For more details, see Appendix 1.

CHAPTER 8

PHASE 5 / MAINTENANCE

Many people come back from a seminar with a binder full of important information. They give it a prominent place on their office shelf — and never look at it again. Once they're back into the swirl of daily decision-making, they feel there's just no time to review and enact the best practices they learned.

The same sort of thing is experienced by some family businesses. They spend time and money on devising and writing a succession plan but rarely go back to it for guidance when succession issues arise, whether those issues have to do with family, ownership, or business. Before long, what's actually happening in those circles is no longer in sync with the succession plan. This can have serious repercussions for a family business, repercussions that may even include having to go through the succession planning process all over again — a time-consuming and expensive proposition.

The Succession Paradigm approach reflects this reality by assuming that changes will occur with respect to the family, owners, and business leadership. Births, marriages, divorces, and deaths are inevitable. So are changes in management, for example, when senior talent moves up or takes on challenges with other companies, or they retire or are terminated. And then there will always be changes in the marketplace that require changes in the business.

THREE CONTROLS

The Succession Paradigm approach controls for these exigencies in three major ways.

First, we work with the family business to create a succession plan that is strong but flexible. We avoid going into details in the plan in a way that hamstrings the leaders. We don't want them to get to the point where they feel it's an all-or-nothing proposition — that they either must follow the plan to a T or ignore it altogether.

Second, we set up a maintenance schedule within the plan that mandates regular reviews of aspects of the plan affecting each circle. This strategy enables the board of advisors and senior leaders to regularly compare business plans against the succession plan.

And third, we set up accountability mechanisms. In the case of Blooms Floral, we scheduled two days of meetings per year. During those two days we had three separate meetings, one with the family, one with ownership, and one with the business.

We scheduled one of the meetings to take place just before or just after the company's annual general meeting. This helped ensure alignment between the leadership's plans and reports, on the one hand, and the vision and goals (including legal and taxation issues) set out by the succession plan, on the other.

The other meeting was set for a month before the annual budget was finalized. We didn't do this in order to go into the details of the budget. Budgets are an operational concern. However, certain shareholder, tax, and legal issues almost always have to be reviewed as companies make financial plans.

Our meetings had two functions.

First, as alluded to above, they checked in on any changes to the family, ownership, or business that might require legal or tax planning changes or structural changes to management.

Second, they measured such changes against the original intent of the succession plan. We made it clear to Blooms Floral that a succession plan can be changed to reflect changes to the family, ownership, and business as long as changes fit the original *intent* of the succession plan. There's no need to hold on to every detail of the original plan if changes do not alter the original purpose of the plan.

We measured the results of Blooms Floral against the objectives established in the plan. We showed the leadership of the company how the maintenance phase was much more than simply getting together to see whether the succession plan was being followed. Rather, this phase incorporated everything leadership had learned from the plan's intense study and research with respect to the family business dynamic and also included new ideas that had developed as a result of ongoing communication with the "new" family business and leadership.

THE PLAN IN ACTION

A year into the maintenance phase — three years into our work with Blooms — the interim president, Sheldon Feinstein, recommended to the owners and the board of advisors that his new VP of US

Operations be appointed president. This was the person he had hired a year earlier as a possible successor. He had determined that neither of Melissa's two older children, Robert and Patricia, was ready for the top spot.

Passing over the main owner's children could have set off explosions in all three circles. But it didn't, because by following the succession plan, ownership and senior leadership had kept everything in the open. The board of advisors had received regular reports from the president regarding the educational and mentorship progress of all three candidates. His recommendation that Robert and Patricia remain in their positions was based not on politics but on the realities of their development. Robert and Patricia themselves, though disappointed, knew this was the right decision. They knew they were still in the running to direct the company from the CEO's chair in the future.

The maintenance phase was not designed to restructure or reorganize the current structure, but rather to preserve its essence. We wanted to ensure that the targets and goals were correct. We then wanted to align those targets and goals and update them accordingly. For example, we knew that leadership's introduction of key new people or development of key new positions would enhance or strengthen the existing culture of the organization. We worked with the CEO to measure such moves against the previous benchmark. In the case of Blooms Floral, the plan and the actuality remained in sync.

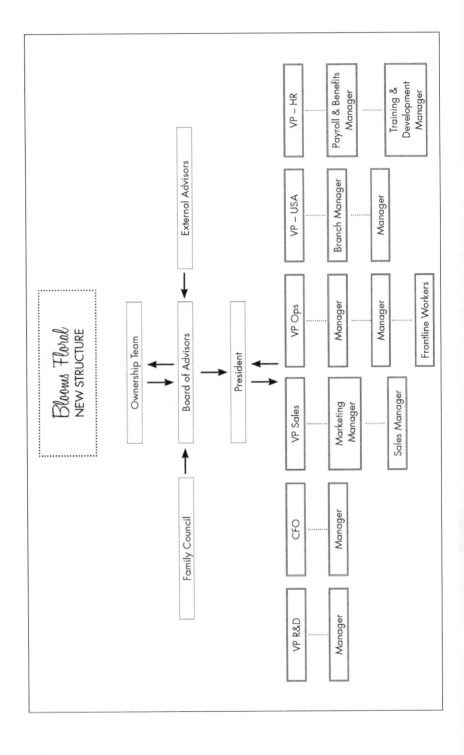

Blooms Floral
NEW STRUCTURE

MEASURING OUTCOMES AGAINST THE PLAN

Our conversations with the leaders of Blooms Floral resulted in a review of opportunities and tasks mandated by the alignment and implementation phases. We asked strategic questions, such as:

» Have you met the plan's objectives?

» Have you provided workable and sustainable solutions?

» Have you succeeded in generating new momentum or clarity in the transition process from the outgoing CEO to the incoming CEO?

» Does the new team complement the new CEO and are the team's strategies in line with modified corporate governance?

» What plans have been put in place to ensure the continued buy-in of those within the company who had not been chosen to lead the company? Should they be given new challenges to ensure their support and growth?

STAFFING

Recruitment is possibly the most difficult task of all. During the maintenance phase, the board assessed the appointments made by the CEO for new positions that had been created by the transformation from the old regime to the new. The board asked:

» Are the appointments succeeding?

» Is the new CEO motivating and stimulating new ideas to energize his team?

» How is HR supporting the development and retention of key staff?

LESSONS LEARNED

As part of the maintenance phase, we conducted a micro-assessment of Blooms Floral, focusing on the new leadership and governance. We asked the new CEO to assess his successes and asked him to rate the overall performance of his key executives. We guided leadership in asking themselves these questions:

> » Have we made any mistakes in recruitment, timing, or any other facet of the succession transformation?
> » Was anyone over-promoted?
> » Was anyone overlooked?
> » Does everyone respect the new leadership? Are people engaged — bringing their energy and passion to the job each and every day?
> » Are things working well under the new leadership?
> » Is the overall transformation called for by the plan proving to be effective?
> » Does everyone know his or her role and how it fits into the bigger picture of the company's overall goal?

Most importantly, we asked whether the new leadership team was having a positive, outcome-based impact on morale and energy, and whether their results were quantifiable. We discussed two crucial issues concerning the CEO and his leadership:

> » Buy-in: Were the CEO and senior leadership buying into the road map and vision for change, and had they made it come alive so everyone in the company was inspired to

buy in? And was ownership buying in? Were they feeling a part of the team and process?

» Sustainment: Was senior leadership providing energy and opportunities for great ideas to flow from the Succession Paradigm plan — ideas that built on the transformation process? Were leaders making changes to the plan that improved it while honoring its purpose and intent?

ONGOING FINANCIAL AND TAX ISSUES

Frank, the minority owner, decided to keep his shares in the company. He liked the new leadership and its vision for the company. He felt that his investment was in good hands and continued to fit his personal financial planning.

Melissa, meanwhile, put her shares up for sale to her three children. Each one bought 30 percent. After consulting the family and her advisors, she put the remaining 10 percent in a family trust for future generations of the family.

All of these moves were made in accordance with provisions of the company's succession plan and were reviewed by the board of advisors.

There was little "chatter" in the family about the leadership's decisions with respect to the Smith children and about the sale of shares. Why? Because everything was unfolding according to plan and all of the lines of communication remained open.

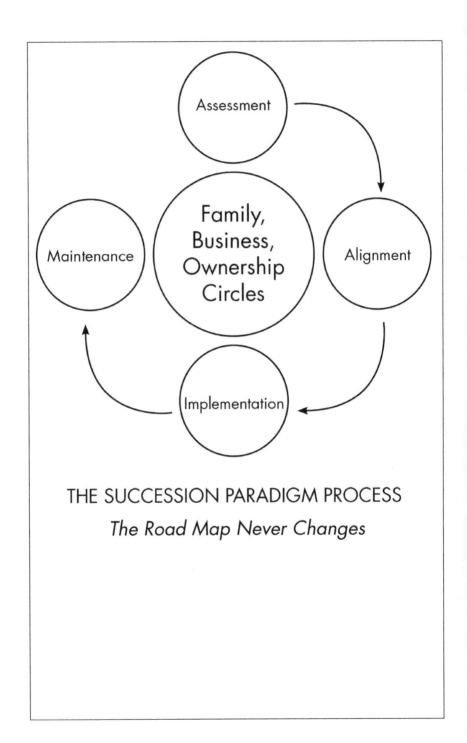

THE SUCCESSION PARADIGM PROCESS

The Road Map Never Changes

. . .

And so it was that the Smith family and Blooms Floral were able to avoid the disasters that so often befall family businesses. Over a three-year period, everyone involved had worked with us to delineate the three circles of the business, determine their own place in the circles, make their own goals and wishes known, and then get their own affairs in order in keeping with the succession plan that was developed.

The Blooms Floral story is not unique. Certainly the planning process was not perfect, whether on the part of those associated with the company or on our part as the Family Business Counsel of Canada team. Nor was the plan perfectly implemented. But in all of the ways that mattered most, everyone involved continued to buy in to the plan.

Melissa and Frank were pleased that their values as owners were still part of the DNA of the company. They felt that their investment was secure and that their values were evident in the company's policies and actions. They were proud of what they had created and pleased with where the company was headed.

Robert, Patricia, and Steve were happy to be contributing to the company's pursuit of profits and increased shareholder value.

And the CEO and senior leaders of the company were confident that they had the support they needed to make Blooms Floral a strong and growing company for many years to come.

FROM A LEGAL PERSPECTIVE

Many people think, "I did my will a few years ago. It's fine." It usually is not fine. Wills and other important documents deserve regular review to ensure that they remain aligned with your needs. Although your financial needs may not change, other things in the will *will* change.

These include the issue of who the trustees and suggested caregivers are for minor children. When your kids are young, you probably chose the grandparents. This is a natural choice and a common one. As the years pass, however, grandparents are often no longer practical choices for this role. So you may have changed your will to indicate that siblings will be the caregivers. Have those siblings moved? Do you want your kids to have to move to another city or country, too? Or if you chose close friends to look after your kids, are they still your friends? If you chose a married couple, are they still married?

The point is that even if your life may be moving forward as expected, the other people in your life may be experiencing more dramatic changes. You must consider such changes and how they could influence your planning.

To put a business perspective on this, family members may sign employment contracts when they join the organization. If they have changed positions, it may be time to revisit those contracts. The contracts may interact with ownership through employee share purchase plans. The ownership may be put out of balance in a family because a child working in the business ends up with a few more shares. Perhaps this child/employee should be excluded from the share purchase plan. Depending on the department the child/employee works in, they may be exposed to confidential information that influences the family and the ownership — information other members may not have access to. You must consider how that makes the latter feel.

The bottom line is that life, the business, family dynamics, and the world around you are in constant flux. Change is inevitable. It is your job to review all of these aspects and determine whether you are still in alignment with the legal documents that govern your relationships and your property.

APPENDIX 1

LEGAL DOCUMENTS

With the three circles that make up a family business come many legal documents. The family, the owners, and the business must use a variety of devices to effect the legal relationships they desire. The purpose of this section is to provide a list of some of the documents that affect each area. Please note that this list is not exhaustive and there is some duplication because some documents may relate to an individual in his or her capacity as an owner *and* in terms of their employment in the business.

FAMILY

» Will — This is the document that speaks from the grave. It determines who will manage your property after you die, how it will be managed, and to whom it will be distributed. It may also suggest potential guardians for minor children

» Power of Attorney for Personal Care — Determines who
will make decisions about your medical care when you are
incapable of doing so. It is often called a "living will" and
may include instructions about keeping you alive (or not)
if you are on life support

» Power of Attorney for Property — Determines who can
make decisions about your property and what kind of
decisions that they can make when you are not capable of
doing so because of mental or physical impairment

» Marriage Agreement — Termed a "pre-nup" by the media,
this is a legal contract between married individuals that
determines property rights and custody rights should the
marriage cease

» Divorce and Separation Agreements — Implemented by a
married couple when they no longer wish to be married.
May include such issues as financial support for each other
and children, division of property, and custody of children

» Employment Contract — Family members employed in
the business may have a formal contract with the business.
This contract not only governs financial issues, it also
includes confidentiality provisions and non-compete, non-
solicit clauses that prevent the employee from working in
a competing business

» Trust Agreement — A legal relationship in which a
person, the testator, contributes property to a trustee who
manages the property for the benefit of the beneficiaries
of the trust. The trustee's responsibility is to act in the
best interest of the beneficiaries and be accountable to

them at all times

» Agreement of Purchase and Sale (estate freeze) — A common transaction that stops the growth of the value of a company in terms of capital gains tax liability to an older generation; this delays payment of capital gains by allowing the growth to accrue to younger generations. As part of these transactions, shares are often sold to various people and entities such as individuals, trusts, and holding companies. These agreements give effect to that sale and include the provisions necessary to ensure tax compliance

» Shareholder Agreement — Discussed in detail at the end of the chapter on Implementation (see page 115) and in Appendix 2 of this book. A shareholder agreement determines many aspects of the relationship between the owners and the company

» Disability Insurance — A policy that pays monthly income to someone when they become incapable of performing the duties of their occupation

» Life Insurance — A policy that pays a lump sum to the beneficiaries of a policy on the death of the insured person. Life insurance comes in both permanent and short-term forms. In the context of the family, it is often used as a tool to fund tax liabilities and replace income

» Life Insurance Trust — A trust that holds life insurance; these trusts are often used in situations in which there are minor or disabled beneficiaries to an estate. Depending on the jurisdiction, they may be used for tax planning purposes, as in the case of an "Irrevocable Life Insurance Trust" in the United States

OWNERS

> » Will — In the context of ownership, the will may include transfer of shares of the business

> » Power of Attorney for Property — The shares of a business may be one of the pieces of property affected by this document

> » Divorce, Marriage, and Separation Agreements — These documents interact with the shareholder agreement

> » Trust Agreement — Shares of a family business corporation are often held in trust, for pragmatic and tax planning reasons

> » Agreement of Purchase and Sale — Also called "estate freeze"; see Agreement of Purchase and Sale, in Family section above

> » Shareholder Agreement — Discussed in detail at the end of the chapter on Implementation (see page 115) and in Appendix 2 of this book. This document comes into particular focus for owners of the business, who are the shareholders

> » Life Insurance (shareholder agreement funding) — Often used to fund the buyout of a shareholder's estate upon the death of the shareholder

» Corporate Will — Discussed in detail at the end of chapter 1; see pages 122–23

» Articles of Incorporation — Documents filed with the government that create the corporation, give it a name, indicate its initial shareholders and directors, and detail the types of shares the corporation can issue

» Articles of Amendment — Changes to the original Articles of Incorporation

» Corporate Minute Book — Stores all of the legal documents regarding the creation, governance, and shareholdings of the company

» Share Registries — A record of who holds what shares

» Lending Agreements with Bank (personal guarantees) — Loans are always formalized with complex documentation. The owners may sign personal guarantees for these loans

» Shareholder Loan Agreement — Formal agreement by which a shareholder lends money to the corporation in relation to pay back, interest, and security

» Lease for Premises — Governs situations in which premises are owned by owners of the business directly or indirectly; often the owners of a business own such real estate through a different entity. The agreement to use the property and the cost of rent should be formalized. This agreement is crucial in situations in which a new owner purchases the business but not the real estate

BUSINESS

» Will — Must be reviewed frequently and revised, if necessary. For example, family members or employees who inherit shares may, as new owners, now become directors of the company

» Employment Contract — Formal contracts with an employee that governs compensation, confidentiality, and whether he or she can work in competing companies

» Agreement of Purchase and Sale — Also called "estate freeze"; see Agreement of Purchase and Sale, in Family section above

» Shareholder Agreement — See discussion at the end of the chapter on Implementation, page 115, as well as Appendix 2 of this book

» Disability Insurance — Companies often fund this insurance for its employees generally or for certain employees. Companies sometimes set up an insurance policy to fund the buyout of a shareholder in case of a disability

» Life Insurance — Companies often purchase "key person" insurance to fund potential reductions in business and replacement costs when a key employee leaves the company or is incapacitated or even dies

» Corporate Will — Discussed in detail at the end of chapter 1; see page 115

» Power of Attorney for Property — This document may be held by someone who has an influence on business decisions

» Articles of Incorporation — Without these, there is no company. Rules concerning who can be directors and how many directors the company has are usually included in this document

» Articles of Amendment — Changes to the original Articles of Incorporation

» Corporate Minute Book — The business is responsible for keeping up to date, on at least an annual basis, this compendium of legal documents regarding the creation, governance, and shareholding of the company

» Lending Agreements with Bank — These documents often affect business decisions because banks often require certain accounting ratios to be maintained. The ability to enter into certain transactions may be influenced

» Shareholder Loan Agreements — Where does the shareholder stand in relation to the bank and other lenders? These agreements will be a determining factor in answering this and other such questions

» Other Banking Agreements — The financial decisions of the business are influenced by all of its account agreements with its bank or banks

» Transfer Pricing Agreement — Governs the prices at which one company supplies another company with common ownership of certain goods or services; especially important with regard to cross-border situations. These agreements are usually reviewed by the taxing authorities of both countries to ensure that both countries get what they perceive as their fair share of the corporate tax pie

» Lease for Premises — This is a key document for certain businesses for which a location is required for them to operate

» Auto Leases — For businesses that lease vehicles for certain employees

» Liability Insurance Policy — Depending on the type of work they do, businesses may take out insurance to cover many types of potential liabilities. These policies often go way beyond the traditional risks of fire, flood, natural disasters, and business interruption

» Auto Insurance Policy — Will have provisions regarding the company's liability in circumstances in which an employee is driving. Provisions may include whether the employee is on duty or not at the time that the liability arises. Employees may have to carry their own policy for certain risks

» Property Insurance Policy — Governs what happens when there is damage to the physical property of the business

APPENDIX 2

SHAREHOLDER AGREEMENTS

When individuals, family members, and advisors engage in a conversations regarding family-owned and -operated business, at some point the shareholder agreement will come up. It is a vital document to understand, whether you are an owner, a want-to-be owner, an advisor, or other. The following will give you a good basic understanding of this important document.

Lawyers are very used to working in a "transactional" environment, and one of the most common documents they implement is the shareholder agreement, an agreement that determines the rules of ownership, the rights of succession, how the shareholders interact with the management of the business, and what happens in the case of catastrophic events. The agreement should address *who* can hold shares and how and under what conditions shares can be sold or transferred and to whom.

Typically, the agreement should supply what are called buy-sell provisions. These provisions outline the circumstances under which one shareholder is obliged to buy shares and another is obliged to sell them to that buying shareholder. Common circumstances are:

» Death
» Disability
» Marital breakdown
» Bankruptcy
» Mental incapacity
» Transfer of shares among the shareholders

DEATH

The death of a shareholder/manager can often mean the end of the business, for several reasons. First, who will manage the business? (This issue is dealt with throughout this book.) Who will buy the shares? Where will the money come from to buy the business? Will they be gifted to family members? What will the tax consequences be? Where will the money come from to pay those taxes?

Think of the following situation, a very common one. A father has trained his son and daughter to take over his business. The business is very profitable and has supported three households comfortably. The children are well equipped to manage most aspects of the business. The business, which Dad built from the ground up, is worth $50 million. Mom died five years ago and Dad never remarried. The children stand to inherit the business.

Dad, however, has never done any estate planning. When Dad passes away, the employees feel certain that their jobs are safe because the children have run the business with their father for several years. But the children get some bad news from their accountant: They did not realize that once they inherited the shares, there would be a huge tax bill. In fact, in Ontario, given that Dad would have a $750,000 capital gains exemption if the shares were "qualified small business shares" under the Income Tax Act, the remaining capital gain would be based on $49.25 million. Applying the then 23.21 percent tax rate to that, the kids owe the government $11.43 million. This is a staggering amount of liquidity for the kids to come up with. What can they do?

> Borrow the money? Now that post mortem expense is at current interest rates, the business can become heavily encumbered

> Bring in a partner? If the children are equipped to run the business, it may not be ideal to bring in another personality

> Shrink the business by eliminating assets? This alternative goes against the very essence of a business: the desire to grow and increase profits

Although the tax implications may be different in other jurisdictions, the problem remains the same. Whether capital gains, estate taxes, or other types of tax, the issue for surviving family members is liquidity. Where do they find the money to pay the tax bill? The simplest and in many cases least expensive alternative would have been for the risk to have been insured earlier. Properly structured life insurance not only may have created the liquidity to fix the problem but also may have allowed the children to take advantage of various provisions of the Income Tax Act.

When the Family Business Counsel of Canada applies all of this to a particular situation, we ask our client to determine whether they have an agreement and examine how it is structured and how it is funded. This is part of the basic fact-finding we do with our clients. In order to determine the right structure for a client, we need to ask such questions as:

» Who are the shareholders (spouses, kids, trusts)?
» Are the shares held directly or through holding companies?
» What type of shares are outstanding (common, preferred, redeemable)?
» What is the fair market value and cost base of shares?
» What does the business do?
   o Active or passive?
» Have owners invested cash?
» Is there a refundable dividend tax account (RDTOH)?
» Has the company been reorganized? What are the details of this reorganization?
» Has the capital gains exemption been crystallized? Are there any exemptions remaining?
» Is there a family trust in the mix?
» Who is married? Common law? Former spouses?
» Are you grandfathered from the stop loss rules?
   o Is there an existing shareholder agreement?
   o Existing insurance?

DISABILITY

Disability is a serious concern in any shareholder agreement. The loss of an active partner can render the business helpless or at least reduce its profitability.

Consider these numbers from the National Association of Insurance Commissioners and the Unum Provident Corporation. A firm with two partners, both thirty-five years old, risks a 67 percent chance that one of those partners will suffer a disability of three months or longer before reaching age sixty-five — far higher than the odds of one of the partners dying before sixty-five. Three partners all forty-five years old run a 90 percent chance of disability.

The insurance-industry research organization LIMRA points out that only 17 percent of the nation's small-business firms (100 employees or fewer) have disability coverage on a partner or key employees. Once a company decides to include such provisions, it must determine how to fund them. There are four options.

1. Cash Method

The business or its owners could accumulate sufficient cash to buy the business interest upon an owner's disability. Unfortunately, it could take many years to save the necessary funds, while the full amount may be needed in a shorter period of time.

2. Installments from Current Earnings Method

The purchase price could be paid in installments after an owner's disability. For the remaining active owners, this could mean a drain on business income for years. In addition, payments to the disabled owner would be dependent on future business performance after the owner's disability.

3. Loan Method

Assuming that the business could obtain a business loan after an owner is disabled, borrowing the purchase price requires that future business income be used to repay the loan plus interest.

4. Insured Method

Only disability buy-out insurance can guarantee that the cash needed to complete the sale, through either a single sum or installment purchase, will be available exactly when needed, assuming that the business has been accurately valued.

Insurance is often a viable option. A buy-out disability policy pays out either in a lump sum or over a period of years (two to five is common), or in a combination of the two. Most policies require a waiting period of twelve to twenty-four months in order to adequately determine that the disabled person will not be able to return, and to prevent healthy owners from prematurely pushing the disabled partner out the door. Choosing a longer waiting period and installment payments will lower premium costs.

Because of the tax consequences and the complexity of buy-sell agreements, you'll want to work with your team of advisors: your financial planner, an insurance specialist, and an attorney, all of whom need to be knowledgeable about buy-sells. Regardless of whether you use insurance or self-fund a buy-sell agreement, you'll need to determine the conditions for a disability buyout, ranging from the price of the buyout, what constitutes a disability, and how long the disability can last before the buyout is triggered. An advantage of using insurance is that the policy defines what constitutes a disability (buy-sell agreements are often vague) and the insurance carrier is the one that determines whether the person meets that disability definition.

MARITAL BREAKDOWN

Marital breakdown is a consideration in any buy-sell arrangement. The concern is multi-fold. First, as a result of property division, a spouse who was not involved in the business could end up own-ing shares. Buy-sell provisions exist to prevent this spouse from ever holding shares. In many cases these provisions also contain general restrictions preventing transfer to a spouse.

In one planning method, a parent excludes from Net Family Property, under the Family Law Act, the shares, and income derived from those shares, that he or she gifts to a child whether by deed of gift or by will. This exclusion is important from a division of prop-erty point of view to protect the family from a spouse who does not want to be part of the business. It also means that the value doesn't have to be divided in case of marital breakdown.

BANKRUPTCY

Bankruptcy is included in a buy-sell agreement so a trustee in bank-ruptcy can never become a shareholder in the business. However, the risk of bankruptcy cannot be insured against. The significant challenge for a business facing a bankrupt shareholder is to provide enough funding to buy out that bankrupt shareholder.

MENTAL INCAPACITY

Issues related to mental incapacity are similar to those of disability. Share transfer is a major concern. Another is the management of the company itself.

TRANSFER OF SHARES AMONG THE SHAREHOLDERS

Shareholder agreements include shotguns, put-calls, and other types of buy-sell provisions. It would take a whole book to outline them all; suffice it to say that a family can let its imagination run wild. There are infinite possibilities in terms of what can happen when one shareholder makes an offer to buy out other ones. Generally, in a family-run business, these clauses are common. Be careful during the drafting of a shareholder agreement that prevents wealthier family members from taking advantage of weaker ones.

FURTHER RESOURCES

Please see our website **www.familybcc.com** for a list of family business and succession planning associations, as well as blogs and websites that deal with family business issues.

In addition, you may find these books helpful:

Built to Last: Successful Habits of Visionary Companies, James C. Collins and Jerry I. Porras. New York: HarperCollins.

Every Family's Business: 12 Common Sense Questions to Protect Your Wealth, Thomas William Deans, Ph.D. Orangeville, ON: Détente Financial Corp.

Generation to Generation: Life Cycles of the Family Business, Kelin E. Gersick et al. Boston: Harvard Business School Press.

INDEX

ABOUT THE FAMILY BUSINESS COUNSEL OF CANADA

The Family Business Counsel of Canada was founded to meet the unique needs of family-owned and -operated businesses. We combine expertise in business management, law, accounting, and insurance with our extensive experience of working in and assisting family businesses.

We also support affiliate relationships with experts across Canada and the United States as they apply our unique process in their assistance of family businesses in their area.

The members of the Family Business Counsel of Canada:

» Michael A. Lobraico is president of the Family Business Counsel of Canada, and president of N.C.I. Solutions Limited. A past president of the Canadian Association of Family Enterprise (CAFE), he speaks on the topic of succession planning for family businesses and assists such businesses with their business planning and succession planning. Having experienced the negative effects of poor succession planning in his family's transportation business, he now helps family businesses separate the three circles of a family business — the family, ownership, and business — and leads them in communicating more clearly within and between circles. Contact: mlobraico@familybcc.com

» Jonathan Isaacs is a founding partner and executive member of the Family Business Counsel of Canada team. He has spent nearly three decades in the life insurance industry and specializes in the use of insurance as a tax planning and succession planning tool. He is a founding partner of the Sabre Insurance Group, and acts as executive vice president for both Sabre Strategic Partners Inc. and Sabre Health Direct Inc., both located in Markham, ON. Contact: jisaacs@familybcc.com

» Mitchell Singer is a lawyer with experience and expertise in tax and estate planning and life insurance planning. In fact, his law degree from the University of Western Ontario includes the special designation Area of Concentration: Taxation. He has worked in the insurance industry since his call to the Ontario Bar in 2000, holding progressive positions with several major insurers including National Life, Canada Life, and Transamerica. He is now the president of Sabre Strategic Partners, Inc., where he oversees operations and works with clients on a daily basis. Contact: msinger@familybcc.com

» Stephen Toale worked in sales management at a major life insurance company for ten years, as well as at two major Investment Dealer Association firms, heading their estate planning divisions both provincially and nationally. He joined Sabre Insurance Group in 2008, where he specializes in insurance-based tax strategies, for companies and individuals. He is a director and executive vice president of Sabre Strategic Partners Inc. Contact: stoale@familybcc.com

» Barry Block is a founding partner of the Family Business Counsel of Canada. He has been a licensed insurance broker in Ontario since 1990. He is a founding partner of Sabre Insurance Group and is president of Sabre Health, Direct Inc. In addition, Barry is a director and executive vice president of Sabre Strategic Partners Inc. He started his career in financial services at Manulife Financial in 1990. Barry's area of specialty is disability insurance, critical illness insurance, as well as life insurance planning to all client profiles. Contact: bblock@familybcc.com

FAMILY BUSINESS COUNSEL OF CANADA PRESENTATIONS

Members of the Family Business Counsel of Canada are available to speak on the subject of family-owned and -operated businesses. Our audiences are primarily made up of people who own or work in a family business or those who serve such businesses — for example, lawyers, accountants, insurance agents, wealth management professionals, financial planners and advisors, Mergers & Acquisitions specialists, and representatives from various industries.

We can provide *you* with:

» Keynote addresses
» Workshops
» Panel discussions
» Facilitated conversations

To inquire about these services, please contact **speaking@familybcc.com**

TO ORDER THIS BOOK AND ACCESS OTHER RESOURCES

Copies of our book *Succession Planning for Family Businesses* are available for purchase from the Family Business Counsel of Canada. Please contact us at **order@familybcc.com** or visit the Family Business Counsel of Canada website.

You can also purchase copies of the book through bookstore websites, including:

 Canada — www.amazon.ca and www.chapters.indigo.ca

 United States — www.amazon.com

 United Kingdom — www.amazon.co.uk

To request updates on the information in this book and to receive other information and articles, please go to the Family Business Counsel of Canada website, **www.familybcc.com**, and follow the instructions there.

www.familybcc.com

CPSIA information can be obtained at www.ICGtesting.com
Printed in the USA
LVOW012055260213

321810LV00007B/26/P

9 781926 645537